Quest

Articles, stories and essays
by a master wordsmith

Russell Frank Atkinson

ISBN: 978-1-922270-80-1 (pbk)
eISBN: 978-1-922270-81-8

Quest

Other titles by the author:

Yoga Pocket Teacher. London: Transworld, 1968.

Basic Biosciences. Sydney: McClelland, 1976.

Your Health: Vitamins and Minerals. Sydney: Doubleday, 1982.

Your Lifestyle: Health and Nutrition. Sydney: Doubleday, 1984.

Modern Naturopathy. Sydney: Harper & Row, 1986.

The Book of Relaxation. Sydney: Simon & Schuster, 1988.

Diary of a Dropout. Sydney: Wellspring, 1990.

A Spirituality for the 21st Century. Zeus, 2008.

Gone Bush. Xlibris, 2009.

Where the Heart is and Dreamscapes. 2018.

ABOUT THE AUTHOR

Russell was born at Portland on the Western slopes of New South Wales in 1930. He started work as a cadet in the advertising department of Farmer's retail store in 1945 and worked subsequently in agencies until he took up the wandering life. Returning to Sydney he discovered Yoga and avidly sought what books were then available. He introduced his peers to Yoga and Indian philosophy and began public classes in Hatha Yoga in 1950, also dancing leads in the first performances of Bharata Natyam in that decade. He taught Hatha and Raja Yoga for many decades, writing the first hand- books on these subjects. He became an assistant to a leading Homoeopath and Osteopath until taking up photography, getting married, siring children and paying off mortgages. Later, he changed vocations again, as an Acupuncturist and Naturopath. He practiced these arts until joining Blackmores in 1975 as Queensland Manager, then in Sydney as researcher, writer, lecturer, and Managing Editor of their Nature & Health magazine. He left in 1983 to go bush for the third and last time.

FOREWORD

Hullo.

Now that you have been adventurous enough to buy a copy of this book I wonder if you know why. I hope that you do; I'm not sure why I wrote it. Maybe it is just a well established habit because I have been writing all my life. It began when I won a short story competition at the age of fifteen which resulted in an offer to join the advertising department of Farmers, a big retail store in Sydney. That was in 1945. A lousy student, I was then repeating second year so I became an office boy and started out on a rocky career in advertising, managing to get sacked twice until finally getting the message that it was not for me, so I shouldered a swag and went bush. But the writing thing endured. I would write descriptions of places and impressions for years to come. It would be so interesting to be able to read them now, so many years later and much to be learnt. Take note would-be writers! Keep whatever you write so you can have the leveling experience of reading your writings decades afterwards. I once found a few pages of verse twenty years old and found the experience so excruciating they were used to ignite the fuel stove.

So here we are in the year 2022. There are now ten books and scores of articles and essays behind me and here I am still at it, posting one or two essays a month to lots of recipients. Writing is what I have done for over seventy years from a spirit of sharing, wonder, joy and love. Many people enjoy reading these postings, which is the reason I keep sending them. After each posting there are encouraging comments or just a 'thank you'. Dr. Edward Todd is one of only two people still alive who knew me in my youth, and whose comments and challenges to my musings, sometimes cause lengthy debates that might become another book. If you get pleasure or benefit from reading this book, please thank Ted who is sponsoring its publication.

Anyhow, here we are, abut to share ideas and musings with a bit of information and whatnot. Blessings be.

Russell Frank Atkinson (Ako)
Published in NSW Australia 2022

CONTENTS

INTRODUCTION

I met the author of this outstanding collection of writings in 1959, when as a migrant youth our employer asked him to teach me the trade and help ease my introduction into the Aussie way of life. It produced revelations and revolutions in my young life. I not only learnt the business but Hatha Yoga, Indian philosophy, Hindu culture and music, Chinese Tao and Japanese Zen, Naturopathy and introduced to the works of Alan Watts, Aldus Huxley, Krishnamurti and Swami Vivekananda - and with that, a whole other way of life. Of course, all that has taken time but that's where it started. Back in '85 I thought to see if I could find my old mentor – and I did, living in a little Tallowwood house called Milkn-honey in a valley on the mid north coast called The Promised Land, so the interchange took a new lease of life.

There is something in **QUEST** for everyone, from the hilarious stories, *Catsh22* and *The Antipodean Pro-Leprechaun Society*, to fine nature writing in *Hampton, Plants* and *Sand Castles* to social commentary in *Upside/Downside* or the interface of Nuclear Science and Indian Philosophy in *Shiva and Science*. So many issues are explored, such as the fact that *Holes are Wholes*, or the eyes, or the Soul, or sex in *Subverting Paradigms* and the mystery of identity in *Who do I You think I am?* Fascinating facts about ordinary old water in *Water* $E=H_2O$ and deep ecological concerns in *A Chat with Mother Nature*. So there is fun to be had, things to be learnt, opinions challenged and the pure pleasure of reading very original prose that sometimes waxes lyrical or is elevated to verse.

Though I sometimes take exception to what I regard as huge leaps in meanings or assumptions that he regards as self-evident but I find obscure, they are nevertheless challenging and evidence of a mind intrigued with the steps of the journey more than affirming conclusions.

Through his regular postings on the internet, I and others have been the recipients of his fertile imagination, cultural concerns, whimsy, and his life-time urge to share knowledge through the written word. So I thought: why don't I publish a selection of these writings to celebrate his ninety-second birthday? So here they are. Revelations and revolutions are sure to be yours too.

UPSIDE/DOWNSIDE

The writings of the French philosopher Rene Descartes upon the prevailing world-view since the seventeenth century cannot be underestimated. Along with the rather brutal approach of Francis Bacon to nature and the world-views inspired by the physics of Newton, Descartes' philosophy gave rise to an almost rigid dualism that has been the characteristic of thinking and attitudes for three hundred years. It was thought that matter and energy, mind and body, God and humans, person and world, were utterly different and that nature and the universe was a vast machine explainable in terms of mathematics. The result of such radical dualism has been almost disastrous, leading, as it has, to the ecological, psychological and cultural problems that now plague us. Obviously, the old mechanistic, materialistic and reductionist frameworks in various disciplines have produced major benefits but there is an escalating downside that also must be acknowledged.

There are few so bold or blind not to admit that our culture is in crisis. Though widely accepted now, it is important to know how come, so by changing our attitudes and ideas as to the true nature of ourselves and the world we live in, the crisis can be changed into opportunity. Those who do not understand the process see society crumbling as the controversies conflicts and traumas escalate, seeing only the negatives; chaos and conflicts. No chicken ever emerged into life without shattering its own egg, no baby the security of the amniotic sac. In the same way we need to break with the old conditioning and so doing, become a catalyst for greater change.

The cause of the situation we now find ourselves in has taken 400 years to develop and can be traced back to world-views promulgated by famous 'natural philosophers' in the days when that term was synonymous with what we now call science. By the mid nineteenth century that world-view was so entrenched that Darwin was reticent in publishing *On the Origin of Species*, not so much because he feared conflict with the Church but that it also pulled the rug out from under the prevailing scientific dogmas of the age that were based upon the notion that the universe was a giant machine whose laws and life forms were fixed from the beginning. The mechanistic, reductionist, dualistic ideas of the Descartian/Newtonian paradigms influenced scientific thinking right up to the present - except in physics, which had to transcend them in order to understand the atomic and subatomic world - nevertheless these paradigms still subtly govern most of our attitudes.

Rene Descartes famous saying 'I think - therefore I am' is revealed as just so much nonsense when it is subjected to the same rational, logical analysis Descartes insisted on as the basis of all reliable knowledge. His declaration is proved false by every human being at least once in every 24 hours, for typical of such divisive dualistic thinking the proposition ignores much of human experience. On the basis of logic applied to his famous saying that the ability to think proves our existence it is fair to assume that when one ceases to think, one would therefore cease to exist – yet each night in deep sleep there is no thought yet we do not cease to be. Though comatose and thoughtless, there is something that continues to exist deep within, giving life and consciousness to all phases of human experience - deep sleep, dream and waking. If one has a need for such affirmations, it is closer to the truth to say 'I exist – therefore I think'

The first dictum isolates the person to the limitations of thought and their being to a personality inside a mechanical body like a ghost in a machine. The reverse dictum makes possible the intuition of a transcendental being behind the mind that exists throughout and gives life to all the three phases of experience. This consideration epitomises the difference between a limited, materialistic, reductionist view of life and the ecological, organic and spiritual, as well as the cause of the many dilemmas we now face.

In the early 19th century, many people hoped that science would bring health, happiness and prosperity to all. Two hundred years later, most people hold the opinion that the scientific method and scientific rationalization has been of unequivocal benefit to humankind. There is now much evidence to the contrary. Taking a wide view that embraces the whole of modern life, including ecology and agriculture, the supposed benefits are certainly not unequivocal.

Nothing can exist in isolation from the culture in which it occurs, and while the early scientists applied their intelligence to discovering facts and sifting truth from old errors, their discoveries were soon exploited by another sort of entrepreneur. Pure science gave way to an acceleration of technologies which made even more exploitable discoveries possible. An uncontrolled escalation of change has been the result as science and technology continued their random developments divorced from moral, ecological, and spiritual values and considerations. *Apart from comforts and some conveniences and undeniable medical advancement, there has been little of real unequivocal benefit to balance the breadth of the problems that have followed in the wake of it all.* It is possible that the price individuals and the ecosystem have to pay for the advantages of much of modern life are too high. The undeniable benefits, mostly medical, have been loudly applauded while the problems have often been down-played or hidden. Yet many once common diseases have been reduced more by better hygiene and sanitation than medical science while 'diseases of affluence' have increased exponentially. Also, most of the real benefits we now tend to take for granted, were brought about by ordinary people getting together to force social and political changes. They were often inspired by religious convictions such as the industrial experiments of the Quakers in the 19th century. In spite of all the modern improvements it is possible that as much suffering has been caused as has been avoided - much of it imposed upon creatures other than human. For every problem science has been lauded for solving, two and more have been created, some taking decades to manifest. *Two hundred years later, the world has been brought to the brink of annihilation more than once and ecological, social, economic, health, personal and moral problems increase each day.* With so many problems and such a high rate of suicides and drug use it must be concluded that society is sick. For this reason, the down-side produced by the old conceptual frameworks within which this civilization functions must be affirmed, and that with emphasis. It is not a matter of a sour reading of things but an attempt to realize an honest appraisal of the situation and current needs.

The causes of the down-side

Sociologists, academics and others have written about the self-centred attitudes in vogue as the result of culture-induced loss of religious faith and the resultant rampant materialism, causing the slavery to machines, the unbalanced worship of the intellect, the idealization of sexual and sensory gratifications, moral and ethical decay lauded as self expression and freedom, social and personal maladjustments, consumerism promoted by manufacturers of unessential possessions and junk foods, ecological disasters and the constant threat of mass destruction.

All these maladies are not due to the application of the scientific method of enquiry into nature, but its misuse, unthinking application and greedy exploitation. Corruption by commerce is rife. Originally the scientific method was applied in an effort to understand nature and the quest for knowledge was inspired by the altruistic love of truth, not for kudos, wealth, fame, power, position or patents, but later became focussed upon control, exploitation and domination. The genesis of the problem is also due to the attitudes of the culture that has applauded and funded it all.

It became the product of the cultural ethos that sees nature as a thing to be dominated, exploited and used in any way we wish. Its pride in itself and its methods, refusing to give any attention, let alone credence, to other methods of knowledge or the more spiritual interpretations of nature, is simply another form of the blind prejudice and dogmatic attitudes of religious fundamentalism. Science and technology are now the Gods universally worshipped, and like every other false God we have built massive pedestals for they must topple and be subordinated to an orderly constraint by higher, non-materialistic values. Nothing short of a spiritual revolution in the mind of the world is likely to be the final solution.

But this can only happen one mind at a time. And time is running short.

Suppositions and facts

Science has as many suppositions and doubtful beliefs as any religion. So much of scientific doctrine is supposition taken as facts. According to the opinions of many orthodox scientists, life began on earth as an accident by the chance catalysis of gases and developed to greater complexity by chance. It then evolved under its own steam through further chance happenings called mutations and adaptations until the series of accidents resulted in Homo sapiens. The sapiens of homo, we are told, is a product of matter, the brain excreting consciousness as the stomach excretes hydrochloric acid.

Humans are merely superior apes, activated by instincts, drives and urges, and their differences and natures are caused by hereditary and environment. At birth their minds are blank slates for these two influences to scribble on. All creatures have evolved through a process of chance mutations, adaptations and 'natural selection.' (Thus denying or overlooking the possibility of a species *intelligent will* modifying its cells or functions to enhance its abilities – a process that might be called *Psychomorphism*). Most of this type of mischief is caused by psychologists, palaeontologists and biologists extrapolating cosmic conclusions from fragmented knowledge.

While no catechisms are chanted daily, these myths and legends, with many ramifications and qualifications, have become the current world-view of the majority, though possibly subliminal, aiding a self-centred materialism.

Science and technology let run amok have been the parents of monsters that threaten, not only death and destruction, but the pollution of the very source of life on the planet. Apart from such a projection of the possible horrors in the future from unbridled development, increasing pollution, chemical, gaseous and electromagnetic, nuclear power plants or warheads, the present excesses beggar the understanding. Billions are spent every day that could put an end to starvation, want and disease, to fund experiments in space and cyclotrons, the results of which will at best, answer some abstract questions of physics and be of no real benefit to anybody.

Inspired by pride in our own abilities, it is now proposed to spend one billion dollars to build a telescope to replace the Hubble. While the science and technology involved is no doubt impressive, it could also be seen to be motivated by a curiosity that is at base, another escape to the false security of even more scientific knowledge.

All worldly attitudes applaud such endeavours. From a humanitarian point of view, such vast sums of money spent on research projects and armaments, when there are so many aching needs that could be relieved or entirely eliminated if a fraction of this amount was spent directly benefiting *people*, is a cause of wonder. It shows where Western culture's values truly are.

The biologist Joseph Needham writing in 1928 epitomises the attitude:

> *Mechanism and materialism lie at the foundation of scientific thought... in science, man is a machine; or if he is not, then he is nothing.*

That sort of thinking is where the crisis comes from.

The upside

All living things are capable of two wonders: self-maintenance and self-transcendence. Contrary to common opinion, civilization and society are also living systems, capable of the same functions as other living systems. In society each unit transcends itself because it contributes to the whole - just as an single cell in the liver does for the whole organ, the organ for the body, the body for the family, the family for the community, the community for the state, the state for the country, the country for the world.

But self transcendence also means the ability of an organism to go beyond its usual limits by going through a period of disorder, instability, even chaos, to immerge with a more flexible and expanded order of functioning. A word for this process is growth; another is revolution.

Those individuals who have dared personal disorder and have transcended it to realize a more stable, organic, integrative, intuitive and spiritual consciousness have contributed to a social disorder that in turn will be transcended as the radical becomes the normal. So the old ways of thought, opinions and attitudes once considered axiomatic are giving away to the new. There are revolutions everywhere.

But the revolutionary changes will take time to become the norm; so will slowly evolve as everything else has. It is much easier to be aware of the escalating problems of the downside than it is to perceive the seeds of radical change germinating in science, all the disciplines and society generally. But the old age with its errors is on the way out. The new age is yet an embryo but is growing fast. To see only the downside is to prophesy doom, but to rejoice in the upside is to be a positive help in the process of onward and upward.

Those who express a vociferous denial of the dangers to all life on the planet by the changes we have made, are impelled by the fear that they are in danger of losing the indulgent life style they regard as essential to the economy and their wellbeing. The great danger is that they can finance powerful lobbyists to block real change, while those who fight for changes or radical reappraisal of current world-views get little attention. The final most disturbing truth might be that this materialistic, technology-driven economy has got itself into a double bind, a blind alley, between a rock and a hard place; a situation in which there can be no *real* solution to the problems modern life has created.

As far back as the 1970's, in largely ignored papers, a few scientists warned about the effects of continued industrial expansion on global warming. They estimated that if it continued at the then current rate that the biosphere would reach its heat limit by AD 2791. Considering that the population and global warming has increased so much since then, this estimate must be much closer to now.

It is true to say that in our long evolution over millions of years, ice ages and all, global warming and pollution by plastics and chemicals in our air, oceans, soil and water is the greatest challenge to human ingenuity, creativity and adaptability our species has ever had to solve.

Even if we do, maybe all we can hope for in the distant future is a reasonably acceptable subsistence. Will old Mother Nature solve the problem in some outlandish and undreamt-of way? Or will the whole structure of what we call civilization come crashing down, putting those who survive back to square one and solve the problem that way? If so it is justice to acknowledge that those few native Australians living close to their traditional life will not have unsurmountable problems.

This was written in 2014.

WATER

E=H_2O

In our civilization water is considered just another commodity to be bought, sold, traded or fought over. It is so much more than a mere commodity or even something essential to life. All great civilizations have been founded on rivers, and in some cases disbanded when the river was no more as happened in India at Mohenjo-Daro when the Sarasvati River changed its course sometime about 1760BC.

The empirical formula can now be written as H_2O but how can two common gasses create the wonder of water? It is unique. There is simply nothing like it. Almost everything is composed of water. Tomatoes are 95% water, potatoes 80%, a cow, 74% bacteria 75% and we humans, 65-70% - more liquid than solid. That seems to be a lot of water, but in molecular terms even more so. 99% of bodily molecules are water. And that water as interstitial fluid is a saline solution akin to sea water. We are sea creatures still.

No other liquid has the properties of water. It verges on the weird. Because it has no taste it is the basis of all our drinks. Filtered through sand for centuries the creeks on Fraser Island have water is so pure it cannot be seen. Everything else in nature shrink when chilled and so does water – until it gets to 4 degrees when it begins to expand until it becomes ice; both bulkier and lighter so it can float on itself. Few things are as perpetually active as a water molecule. A glass of water seethes with activity as molecules dance about changing partners billions of times a second. Why and how is unknown; there are over seven theories about it which underscores the fact. So you see, though it seems so, there is no such thing as a body of still water. A seemingly still glass of water also has currents, columns and hides different types of water molecules and two different phases of water. Close to the glass the water has a negative charge while the adjacent water is positive. This negative water is highly weird. It excludes particles, so early researchers called it the Exclusion Zone, EZ. Little was done to investigate it until the work of leading researcher Gerald Pollack revealed its wonders. The science shines light on many of the obscure properties of this little molecule. It also shows up the faulty scientific dogmas that have had universal acceptance that attempted to explain such things as why vapour rises off hot liquids, ice formation, why gels don't leak, endless bubbles rising from Champagne, why is ice slippery, why ships float, how water gets to the top of tall trees, what are bubbles, drops and vesicles, why do some things repel water, why does water vapour have such cohesive force that some forms clouds and how can huge rain clouds float in the air and drift on the breeze though they weigh megatons, how can some creatures walk on it and why can stones be made to skip over it? Satisfactory explanations have been rare. All may be due to the presence of the EZ.

One unexpected result of this difference in charge between negative EZ and positive water is that it can cause of flow of electrons. A small bottle of water can power a digital clock. How did the ancient Egyptians split the huge stones to build the pyramids? With water of course. They had plenty of it so they soaked wooden wedges driven into the stone with plenty of water and waited awhile. The expanding cells split the stone. Water is the stuff of magical illusions and though the molecules stick firmly together to make oceans they will obligingly separate if you dive in and are adhesive enough in contact with air to let the South American Jesus Christ lizard walk on it and stones skip.

In our arrogant ignorance we have given this poor old planet a hard time. We have even misnamed it. Considering the importance of water to life itself and the fact that most of its surface is covered in it, the planet should have been called Aqua. This simple little triangular molecule of H_2O is a marvel and a wonder. It seems to defy the laws of chemistry and physics – it expands when frozen, floats on itself, can be induced to flow against gravity and is the universal solvent. Without it no life could have appeared on the frightful seethe of the molten earth. Biologists have reckoned that it takes 100 tonnes of water to produce one tonne of plant life. Seventy five percent of that plant weight will be water in transit. In a sense water can be regarded as the prime nutrient for without its dissolving powers other nutrients would have no vehicle, seeing that the chemical reactions which manifest plant and animal life can only occur between substances in a solution of water. Eventually, though it may take 2000 years all the water on the planet will take part in the process of photosynthesis.

Water is the spirit of humility. Though it has no colour of its own it reflects all others. It takes the shape of whatever container it is put into; has no taste but carries all others. It has no form of its own and flows away from high places, seeking the lowly. Uncontaminated, it is as unseen as air. Void of voice, it tinkles, gurgles, chimes, roars or thunders. Humbly flowing around obstacles it will also wash them away. It is the bringer of life and death. Amazing stuff; it should be worshipped and treated with great respect.

Christians acknowledge something mystical about water at the baptismal font and with gestures and prayers convert tap water into holy water. Hindus revere water as God, so not only is the Ganges considered holy. Hindu rituals make great use of water and water used as oblations is often taken as medicine. In temples there may be a bowl of water at the shrine with a long handled spoon. The holy water is spooned to the palm of the hand and sipped. Pagans too, revered water; a boon to modern anthropologists who find a treasure trove of objects in the bed of old waterways, ponds and lakes once ritually offered to the spirit of water.

According to the principles of homeopathy, water has the ability to absorb the subtle - and therefore the most potent – nature of therapeutic substances when the right method of preparation is followed. This can be triturated to such an extent that a homeopathic medicine can have a therapeutic effect if properly prescribed though an analytical chemist could not detect one molecule of the original substance. Water is magic stuff.

So magical that research into its properties has resulted in scientific controversies that have adversely affected the careers of quite a few. So much so that it has been an unpopular field of scientific study until the recent work of Gerald Pollack, whose research has solved some anomalies and revealed the weakness of accepted theories, most of which just don't hold water. Even so, with the use of cutting edge technology there is still much in doubt. This fact is as amazing as water itself, for this simple little molecule has been subject to scientific study for hundreds of years, yet still defies a final understanding of its properties.

Giorgio Piccardi (1895-1972) was puzzled why reaction times varied so much in various experiments involving water, though all extraneous influences were eliminated and methods strictly followed. His lab conducted nearly a quarter of a million experiments over twelve years, finally concluding that some sort of external energy must be responsible. Detailed analysis revealed that results followed a yearly cycle repeated year after year. He also noted that reaction times varied in accordance with solar activity, especially with sunspots and flares. Decades later Simon Shnoll in similar biological experiments concluded that geophysical and cosmic forces were responsible for the fluctuations in experimental data. This was confirmed when Vladimir Voeikov's work revealed that cosmic events were certainly involved as he recorded the effects upon water of a local lunar eclipse and the phases of the moon.

All this scientific data demonstrating the incredible sensitivity of water's little molecule must have huge and unknown repercussions upon every living thing. Our sixty million bodily cells are mostly water. What are the implications of all this?

The research of Masaru Emoto into water's therapeutic potentials merges on the mind-boggling, for its shows that water not only dissolves substances but is also capable of holding information and is influenced by many external influences. To prove this, he has exposed beakers of water to music, and words both spoken and written and can show various repeatable responses. This is a way-out and unacceptable conclusion yet seems to be unexplainable any other way. In order to show this he freezes the water until it forms crystals and then photographs the crystals, which vary depending on the influence. Harmonious influences of any kind produce beautiful balanced crystals but inharmonious ones produce unbalanced or even ugly shapes and some not at all. Emoto has devised a method of treating water in specific ways to match the energetic nature of people suffering from a range of maladies with outstanding success. The methods, experiments and case histories are the subject of his many books. As other researchers have proved, he found that sunlight gives water energy and produces excellent crystals; which should be no surprise.

The leading Russian researcher, Vladimir Voeikov, has exposed a beaker of water briefly to the sun and then put it into a dark cupboard. Tested at intervals, it has radiated light continually for twelve months. I have long suspected these properties and for many years have put water or wine in the sun to 'get charged' as I say. So I get to drink extra harmonious liquids. The nature of the water we drink has an enormous influence on our mental and physical health. Most of us are drinking dead water little exposed to light; whatever else might be wrong with it. It's worth putting some glasses out in the sun each day to help build the EZ and get charged. Sing it a happy song or tell it how much you appreciate it. Just like all of us, water doesn't like of being mistreated, ignored or taken for granted. There is something very human about these little molecules.

THE ANTIPODEAN PRO-LEPRECHAUN SOCIETY

It is little known that I used to be the Founding President of the exclusive Antipodean Pro-Leprechaun Society. It convened every Friday evening in rooms behind a restaurant in Crow's Nest, a north shore suburb of Sydney. It is fitting then, that our symbol was of a crow on the edge of its nest feeding a Galway sausage to a leprechaun.

So exclusive was this society that members were limited to nine as this number of all numbers is a magic leprechaun-type number. This too, is a little known fact, but if you care to get pen and paper and do the numbers you will discover that however you multiply nine the resultant is always back to nine – like this – 9+9=18; 1+8=9, and so it goes. Members know that it achieves these unusual properties because nine represent a trinity of trinities; three threes, and that trinities are the foundation of everything. But in saying this I must be careful not to give any of our secret knowledge out. Nevertheless, I can reveal that membership was also restricted to those who answered NO to the following legend.

There is a distant planet covered with a magic forest in which not one creature exists, not even a microscopic mite: certainly no animal or human. There is nothing in this forest except plants and huge trees. The oldest tree is massive, the trunk like a tower and the branches immense. One day this tree fell. *Question:* did this giant tree crashing to the ground make a noise?

A YES answer disqualified a prospective member for what must be obvious reasons. Not only that, but inducted members had to memorize the following liturgy which we chanted lustily at the start of proceedings:

Once upon a timeless, everything that ever was, was an is. All the is was spontaneous joy which flowed from moment to moment with such intensity that there wasn't space for the past or the future because everything happened at once. So of course, everything was always new because there couldn't be a twice. Sure, and so it is it is. Except to say, that is, that once upon a timeless, everything that ever was, is, or was to be a That and it flowed from nowhere to nowhere, just like an is.

What a marvellous sight it was to see us all singing and dancing in our green vests and yellow knee breaches, waving our tasselled caps and quaffing tankards of Guinness. When I sounded the gong we all took out our Dunhill pipes and red and yellow tins of Erinmore Flake pipe tobacco, lit up with our Dunhill lighters and puffed away while we told stories of ancient kings, ruined castles, great warriors, of peatbogs and craggy mountains high in mystic mists, wild sea shores, manses and sodhouses. Of wily witches, wizards and warlocks - but of course, mostly of the mischievous antics or heroic deeds of the Little People.

Such a marvellous evening was finally brought to a close by us toasting each other with a dram of Tullamore Dew. The ritual was most impressive, as we stood unified by interlocked arms and solemnly chanting, to the tune of J.C Bach's cantata Weinen, Kladen, Sorgen, und Zagen BWV12

Twinkle twinkle little star, how you wonder what we are, up above the sky so low, toodelloo, it's time to go.

Then, changing into our business suits we made our merry exits through the back door to the line of waiting taxis. But that was long ago, and I am the last of them. All the others have succumbed to various misadventures, heart attacks and liver disease. Living longer, I have had the benefit of the latest technology so am now recuperating from a liver transplant donated by a teetotaling Seventh Day Adventist to whom I am grateful - though it would have been my pleasure to inform him that in an ideal world the week should be of nine days, not seven.

SANDCASTLES

Four hundred thousand years ago, sand, spiraling up through the surf from way down south, began to pile up off the coast of Queensland.

Who knows now, the concatenation of forces, currents, or accidents, some perhaps reaching out into the cosmos, causing these sand islands below the Tropic of Capricorn?

Perhaps it was piles of pumice stone spewed out from the cluster of volcanoes whose jagged cores rise lofty above the coastal flats on the mainland that trapped the sand so long ago. As the sands built up above the tides, the first to come were the sea birds resting. It wasn't long – a few thousand years maybe, that the sand piles were fecund islands with ecosystems all their own; forests, lakes, lagoons, wetlands and vibrant heaths. Kangaroos, wallabies, dingoes, and emus waded over the sand drifts or maybe as adventurous as Columbus or Magellan, swam out to discover new worlds.

Then humans came to give everything a name. They called the oyster Ningi, the fern whose tuber they ate, Bungwahl, the hardy little tree of knobby grey bark and brittle spiky leaves that rattle in the wind, Wallum. White skinned people who now live on these islands have their own names for everything, but they call the heath lands by its old aboriginal name. It's a good name for the hardy, prickly little plants of the Wallum. Like the tree, the Wallum is without grace, but is of great character.

From the ancient spirit of the island's point of view, we knew humans are queer creatures indeed. It resents our intrusion. We have asphyxiated the earth with smothering of cement and asphalt, run cattle over it. Men in suits have developed whole creeks and wetlands out of existence and felled the diverse forests to plant huge areas with pine – a tree the island's creatures have little use for, except as a perch for an exhausted parrot looking for an old gum with a nesting hole in it.

The ancient spirit, sharp as sand and as magical as a silicon chip, does not inhabit the entire island anymore, for where the new humans have gathered, the spirit departs. Yet in some places, if you stand very still, intently listening, you may hear the echo of its chanting. The old spirit comes about as soon as I get beyond the sound of a car, down one of the tracks into the Wallum or into the sand flats behind the beach near where Mathew Flinders had a run-in with the locals, so he called it Skirmish Point. Here for reasons I wonder at, are hectares of undulating sand covered mostly in spinifex. Way back from the beach it meets a sharp rise where the scrub starts; gums, wattles, banksias and tea trees, nothing over three meters high. Bonzied, I guess, by dryness, salt winds and sand where they battle it out in true Aussie style, too thick to walk through.

The old spirit chants its soft self-obsessed song here over the muted sound of the Pacific beating into the bay up the channels off Morton Island. It tells me that the rise was once the first of the dunes not so long ago (as time with old spirits goes) and that the sea came into a deep bay here where the Dugongs fed on the sea grasses and the aborigines netted them in the season according to the totem.

Behind the soft slow chanting in this lonely place there hums a primal silence. There is little visible life in this arid place, though I can see rows of little indentations in the sand where a sand-coloured crab has wandered about exploring far beyond its hole, so laboriously dug.

Sometimes I amuse myself following their wanderings, wondering what the funny little sideways creatures, eyes up on stalks, had in mind when they suddenly turned left or right, or circumnavigated a hillock instead of seeing what gives from up on top. How, I wonder, do they see their hole from such a distance? Eyes on stalks must be a help, but it doesn't explain the beeline accuracy with which a startled crab gets home.

The south-east tip of the island is covered in the original forest of Eucalypts and coastal scrub where I first saw the beautiful Bee-eaters with their long slim tails and the bright red Mistletoe birds who, after gobbling the fruits, wipe their bums free of the sticky seeds on high branches, insuring plenty of Mistletoe fruits for future generations.

When the tide is out by the mangroves on the channel side of the island, the crabs get the spirit of adventure and hundreds explore down to the water's edge sampling delicious bits of detritus, shovelled into the mouth one claw after the other. But come me, thirty meters or more away and ZAP! Back they go, four legs sideways down their own personal burrows. How they do the four legs sideways thing without tumbling over is another wonder.

After many experiments, I have not seen any indication of confusion about what hole belongs to which crab. By the time I get to crabsville, walking the beach in the gloaming, there is not a crab to be seen. If I stand still awhile, a crab appears at the mouth of its hole, four legs in, four legs out. Then another and another; eye stalks doing the full 360.Then comes the tentative amble, but the slightest movement on my part and the beach is crabless again.

Crabs are smart little intelligences that have come up with the idea of putting their skeleton on the outside. This is one reason they still inhabit the planet with an ancestry going back to the Beginning. But just how good is a good idea in the long run? Putting the skeleton on the outside has insured for the crustaceans a permanent place on the rollcall of life forms but has fixed forever their lowly place on the ascending spiral. C'est la vie.

No matter. One can be sure that one of the first creatures to take up residence on these old islands were crabs, who have been busy cleaning up the detritus ever since the island was a sand bar.

RELIGION AND THE NEW SPIRITUALITY

When social groups meet there is usually an understanding, explicit or implicit, that there are two subjects that should be excluded from debate - or even comment. It's no news to anybody that the subjects are religion and politics, and it is likely that spirituality new or old would be included. It could be argued that these epistles are a sort of electronic get-together but without sanctions or agreement as to their content. Therefore, all taboos aside, here is an email that includes them all, religion, politics, spirituality and then some. The content may not be of great interest, though we are all seekers of something we know not what and maybe this will lead you to the 'what'. The rapid growth of interest in Yoga and a spirituality free of dogma and belief systems in the last fifty years has been phenomenal and indicates a major trend in the evolution of consciousness. So much so that there are now millions of people engaged in various methods of Self-knowledge and experience freedom from the tyranny of erroneous ego-driven thinking. There is a new spirituality slowly seeping through the old.

In this paradoxical Universe here is another paradox: What may be regarded as the new wave of spirituality sweeping the world is in fact ancient. Sometimes it wears its old traditional clothes, at others a very different garb. Its source is Indian philosophy where it was called Advaita, meaning non-dual, contrasting it to the popular dualistic religions in vogue all over the world. Its influence began trickling into the Western world in the 18th century, flowing in the 19th and 20th centuries and now quietly filtering through every nation and culture.

Advaita Vedanta is a non-dualistic philosophy so all-encompassing that it does not deny dualistic religions but integrates them into a higher understanding. It regards dualistic religions and philosophies as being necessary steps to a unified knowledge, just as the 'old science' has been to the startling new science of quantum theory. In a similar fashion quantum physics grew out of Newton's physics and the one really significant difference between them according to Sir Arthur Eddington, is that quantum physics has been forced to acknowledge that it does not deal with an ultimate reality. The Vedantic view is that duality is the temporal world experience projected by the mind upon an eternal non-dual, ultimate reality. So the apparent duality is based upon a non-dual reality. This is the fundamental principle of the ancient Vedanta.

When opposites are regarded as absolute and duality rules, knowledge is divided into apparently conflicting principles. How does mind relate to matter? Matter to energy? Man to nature? God to man? Man to God? And so on. In the light of Vedanta, Western philosophy and science have struggled to bridge gaps that don't really exist; to unify parts of a single body and reconcile differences between opposites that are only apparent. This mental attitude was the main block to understanding the strange things that arose from the experiments of atomic physics and had to be given up.

Atheists are people who think that they *know* that God *doesn't* exist; theists are people who think that they *know* that God *does* exist. These opinions are only about ideas. God is the name of the unknown.

The Absolute is not that which is conscious of the internal world, nor that which is conscious of the external world, nor that which is conscious of both, nor that which is sentient, nor that which is simple consciousness, nor that which is insentient. It is unperceived, not related, incomprehensible, un-inferable, unthinkable, and indescribable. ...The Supreme is not to be fixed; it is unlimited, unborn, not to be reasoned about, not to be conceived.

...You cannot see That which is the Seer of seeing; you cannot hear That which is the Hearer of hearing; you cannot think of That which is the Thinker of thought; you cannot know That which is the Knower of knowledge. This is your Self that is within all. Everything else but This is perishable.

...That alone know as God and not that which people here worship. That which cannot be apprehended by the mind but by which the mind is apprehended – That alone know as God and not that which people here worship. (Selected from the Upanishads)

Spirituality is to feel the reality of a Great Mystery or Supreme Being, different to the God of religions, and feel it with a sense of mystery, awe and wonder. It is an important, even essential, aspect of being truly human. It is possible that some atheists have more of this feeling than some theists.

To theists, such a feeling tends to bring in its wake an ego-flattening and arrogance-inhibiting humility, and has an integrating effect on the psyche, fostering a responsible attitude to others as members of a family under the fatherhood (or motherhood) of a cosmic parent, or in the case of altruistic atheists, humanistic concerns which provide a ground for fellowship, love, unselfishness, morals and ethics.

The belief in a higher reality can be beneficial because it helps to integrate the personality into a place in the universe and into itself, though it is not a matter of mere belief, but of a deep intuitive feeling. On the other hand, ordinary materialistic atheism tends towards disintegration if it asserts that life is a fortuitous accident, that consciousness is a product of matter, and that the individual human is merely a smart animal and a product of chance, genes and social conditioning. These are the disintegrating factors that make the individual into an isolated unit in an unsympathetic and antagonistic universe – a lonely, isolated ego in conflict with nature and in competition with all others. These are the erroneous ideas that inform much of the 21st Century angst, neurosis and psychosis. The Advaita spirit is not to regard dogma and belief systems as the core of religion but rather as a starting point to understanding verities that should be ultimately transcended. It accepts the concept of God but does not demand a belief in any, because it understands the significance of the idea of God, and respects it. I think that in millennia to come, it will be the common understanding. Philosophically, its major influence in the world is through Advaita Vedanta and scientifically through the concepts of theoretical physics that are tending towards a non-dualistic reality at the core of the Universe. Einstein has expressed it in two different ways, one personal and the other scientific –

'A human being is part of the whole called by us the 'Universe', a part limited in time and space. He experiences himself, his thoughts and feelings, as something separate from the rest – a kind of optical delusion of his consciousness. This delusion is a kind of prison for us, restricting us to our personal desires and to affections for a few persons nearest to us. Our task must be to free ourselves from this prison by widening our circle of compassion to embrace all living creatures and the whole of nature in its beauty. Nobody can achieve this completely, but the striving for this achievement is in itself a part of the liberation and a foundation for inner security.' *The New York Post,* 28 November 1972.

He has written:

'We may therefore regard matter as being constituted by the region of space in which the field is extremely intense...there is no place in this new kind of physics for both the field and matter, for the field is the only reality.' Again: 'The field exists always and everywhere; it can never be removed. It is the carrier of all material phenomena...It is the void out of which the proton creates the pimesons. Being and fading of particles are merely forms of the motion of the field.'

It is heartening to see that due to these influences there is a growing spirituality of a different sort. It is now widely accepted that one can live a spiritual life without having a specific religion.

For most of us, getting a clear understanding of the significance and role of religion is difficult, because the major religions have become compromised by cultural and political issues. So much so, that these influences are commonly regarded as essential to the religion itself. Simply put, religion is an acknowledgement of the spiritual nature of relationship to one another and to a super cosmic intelligence that makes life possible. This is the core of all religions and can be expressed in many ways depending upon national culture and its spiritual and intellectual development. Consequently, the leading religions being old are overlaid with redundancies. They worship many other things, which may include privilege and hierarchy, history, prejudice, buildings, wealth, insularity, doctrines, and the various cultural and political overlays that have often eclipsed the simple core of the religion with a tough outer shell. Religion has been done a great disservice by the minority who use religion as a hook to hang their fears, insecurities or neuroses upon. They tend to be fanatics; people over-compensating for secret doubts and insecurities, and the religious variety of bigots, like fanatics, are so because they lack a real understanding of their religion or have a severe lack of sympathy and empathy which religion should inspire.

True religion is more a matter of relationship, not of dogmas, belief systems, rules and regulations.

Different opinions within each religion create schisms; governments, individuals and movements then amplify and exploit the resulting divisions for economic or political advantage. At the present time such exploitation has become the major cause of conflict and wars, but such events are not the natural outcome of religion itself, for in many cultures major religions have co-existed without conflict for centuries. The prevalence of conflict has caused many people to disparage religion and turn to sectarianism and attitudes of rational expediency; reminding me of an old saying about taking care not to throw the baby out with the bath water. Another aspect of this confusion is the tendency to deny the possibility of there being a God because of the horrors that are due to nothing else but the acts and motives of individuals who have no real spirituality, even if religious. 'Shit happens' is a very graphic allusion to this and very apt as shit if the outcome of what we ourselves have cooked. Every religion that ever was and is worthy of the name, has insisted upon an ethical, moral, gentle, loving life. But nations and governments, in order to be strong, are by necessity unethical, immoral, martial and given to expediency, in spite of rhetoric to the contrary. The national religions are thus bent to political ends.

Contrasted to conventional religions based upon the belief in dogma, faith and traditional practises and rituals, those who are part of the new spirituality may have little or nothing to do with such things. By study, contemplation, discipline and meditation they seek to realize within themselves their unity with all life and hence, their responsibility to God, others, the world and nature. It is not an easy task. It is a living, individual thing with no fixed form as its adherents may or may not be affiliated with a society, organization or group. Their attitudes being truly catholic, some may be active in different societies, religions or groups. Some are active in society and some not. A few are leaders within the folds of a religion working from within it to broaden its mindset, supporting interreligious meetings and dialogues. This worldwide movement is largely due to the influence of Vedanta. Most of those influenced by the new spirituality are students of Oriental philosophy and practitioners of one of the forms of yoga or similar methods and teachings.

A great teacher of Vedanta philosophy and spirituality often contrasted the ordinary person to a soggy matchstick. Just as we all have within us the spark of divinity, it cannot come to light as no matter how often a soggy match is struck it cannot ignite. The spiritual life is an attempt to get rid of the sog; so when struck, the spark can become a flame. The seekers of an ultimate understanding, though leading a quiet, unobtrusive life can realize astounding revelations in the light of the flame. It is a difficult, sometimes tedious job; one reason it is not popular. Hidden or active, the influences of such intrepid explorers are like leaven in the mind and soul of the world. Even remote and inactive, they inspire every change for the good.

That sounds rather grand, so it is important that readers don't assume that I include myself as one of these august individuals. Rather like a tourist who plans to visit a certain country, studies its culture, consults maps, reads its history and collects as much data about it as possible, so have I about Yoga, Vedanta, Zen, Buddhism and Oriental culture. As far as touring the actual country is concerned, I have not even begun to begin. With that erroneous supposition out of the way, herewith the end.

PS. There is plenty of information about Vedanta on the internet and YouTube and some on Advaita.

REALITY IS RIDICULOUS

One of the most amazing sights in the universe is a human on a horse. When the two-legged one gets on the back of the four-legged one, it is a miracle to wonder at. When the big, more magnificent one does whatever the small less handsome one wants, it is well-nigh unbelievable. Dressage is the incredible perfection of this combination of animals. Because I have this sort of attitude to humans on horses, humans on elephants, camels or emus leave me speechless. Man on horse is very ordinary to us, but it wasn't for the Aztecs. There were no horses in the Americas, so the Aztecs never got the idea of putting one animal on top of the other for purposes of locomotion.

When Aztecs first watched Cortez unload horses from the ships they were afraid and amazed, hiding in the forest. When they saw the humans astride the four-legged creatures they made off to tell Montezuma that Gods with six legs and two bodies had come. Naïve as they were, they saw something that Cortez and his men were blind to. The commonplace is marvellous, and everything is extraordinary. It's good fun to see things this way – and here is a strange thing - it is not by flights of fancy and imagination, but by seeing things as they really are.

If it is possible to get over or under or around our conditioning and see things with new eyes, it's a laugh a minute and worth throwing your old self away to get there. As an example, consider your attitude to a symphony orchestra, which you probably regard as an august affair of much decorum. And so it is, but it is also bizarre in the extreme if you look at it as it is. Here is what really happens.

A select group of animals that refer to themselves as humans and give themselves top marks on that account, sit on a raised platform. Other humans sit on seats in rows. The select group has trained for years to play with a strange assortment of objects. Some are wooden boxes with the entrails of cats stretched from end to end that are scraped with a bow made from the tails of horses. Others have an amazing assortment of metal tubes twisted in all sorts of convolutions that they put in their mouths and blow down. The biggest object is a wooden box with hammers attached to keys that are pounded with the fingers that cause others to hit wires stretched on a metal frame. Other wires stretched on other boxes are plucked. Behind them is a man surrounded with tubes that have the skins of other animals tightly stretched over the tops and metal disks that dangle off a stand. In each hand he holds a stick which he bangs on the top of the tubes or on the metal disks.

A man dressed in formal evening wear that makes him look like a Penguin, stands in front and waves his arms about as they all blow, scratch, bang and pluck and the other lot listen to the noise they all make. Then when they are finished something really strange happens. The ones who were listening to the noise bang their palms together and make a nasty noise back.

Reality is ridiculous and everything is too amazing to take seriously. The Gods are laughing fit to kill. No scientific explanation is ever likely to be preposterous enough to account for it.

What if life is nothing but a brilliant joke dreamed up by a hilarious God, and you are no more than a figment of your own imagination? Chills some of us to the bone, that does, but I for one like the idea. It seems to make anything probable and everything possible.

The mundane is amazing. Right now for instance, how many people in so many different settings are evacuating the residues of yesterday's dinner? Putting the food in might have been done in company with degrees of ceremony; even pomp, but the inevitable outcome is done behind closed doors and all alone. That's funny enough, but what if it was done the other way around? How strange it is that twice a day almost every human on the planet abrades their teeth with plastic bristles in a mouth full of chemical froth? Consider the weirdness of another ordinary activity usually done secretly and in pairs. It is hard to think of a human activity as bizarre as the strange rite of sex. Biologically considered, it is a weird and ingenious method of mixing gene pools, but when complicated by the psychology, emotions and romance we have invested it with, it becomes ludicrous. When everything is seen as weird as it really is, reality becomes ridiculous and good for a laugh.

THE MIGHTY METAPHOR

"Mother! Mother! My boat is sinking here in the ocean of this world. Fiercely the hurricane of delusion rages on every side! Clumsy is my helmsman, the mind: stubborn my six oarsmen, the passions: into a pitiless wind I sailed my boat and now it is sinking!"

From the Gospel of Sri Ramakrishna page 155.

Sages and gurus have often used this oceanic metaphor to help us realize the fact that we are afloat on an ocean of life and are tossed about on waves of tears and laughter, ennui and excitement, success and failure. Freedom means to cross this tempestuous ocean of life and arrive safe and sound on the other shore. To do this help is needed, for though we may be sure that we are going in a certain direction, the whole body of water we float on might be moving in another, while we go up and down with the waves and back and forth with the tides.

No two of our little boats are the same. The variety of hull, cargo and rigging is beyond computing and all these vessels sailing the ocean of Now, no matter what their course, are floating on currents that will take them all unerringly to the abyss of the unknown where time comes to a stop; the edge of the world we know, where the ancient mapmakers printed HERE BE DRAGONS. We now know there are no dragons, as one day in distant time we will know that the fear of life and death is likewise a product of limited knowledge.

Surely, seeing our life as sailing on oceans of time to a distant shore or inevitable edge is an appropriate metaphor. There are sharks in the water and pirates afloat to spice the journey though we blow most of the ill-winds out of our own mouths and those who are convinced that they know the right course for us to sail on, and insist we do so, are the cause of most of the storms. Those who try to direct the tides, winds and currents cause most of the bad weather. Gales of greed, hate and fear are tempests that drive whole fleets into whirlpools of destruction.

Deeply considering the nature of the mighty metaphor and knowing the capabilities of boat, cargo and rigging, the sails can be unfurled to go explore new worlds. But where is the other shore? Like Columbus, we do not know if it exists. Perhaps there is no land at all, so we sail on and on, round and round on a global ocean; water without end, fated to sail on for all time. Young life-lovers might think this was grand but we sea-sick ancients hope for a homeport where we can jump ship.

Down this current of time
Sailed I for eons
Through minutes, hours, days, lifetimes,
Worlds,
Down, down,
Winding ways
Surging with the times' tide
An ever flowing I.

I
A builder, laying
Tomorrows' foundations.
A painter of thoughts,
Mind the canvas,
Or a sculpture,
Life the stone,
Each act a blow
Upon the chisel,

As a skipper of a paper boat,
We sail the seas
Of storms and tranquil waters.
Engrossed as a child
We play in each,
Not knowing that
Each second is tot-ter-ing,
Tot-er-ing, Tot-er-ing,
On the brink of eternity:
The ever-present Port.

With a little imagination moralistic parables flow like water. I imagine that it is wise to float lightly on the tossing waters taking care that all the water stays outside your ship; allowed inside it is possible to drown in your own boat. Avoid floundering by taking proper care of the hull and sails and keen intelligence and care-less faith are best on the helm. Some ships become so top heavy and have so many armaments that they capsize. Some get so sea-sick they scuttle themselves but sometimes satgurus as powerful tugs tow many craft straight across to the other shore. Winds of desire push most ships about on collision courses. Boarded by a pirate you may not only be robbed but made to walk the plank. There are many storm-torn old ships near the brink, sails of purpose blown away.

Gently drifting
Void of intentions,
No sail, oars nor rudder,
No need;
The current takes
The steer-less craft
Unerringly across the seas
To world's end.

I wonder; are we fated to a fixed course unsuspecting, thinking all the time that we are the navigator? Of the vast variety of boats sailing the seas did we inherit our hull, masts and rigging or did we build it all ourselves? All the creatures alive with us in a bewildering variety of shapes and sizes must be craft too, sailing towards the same edge of death. Are our past acts the winds that drive us as well as the weather shared by all? Are there distant islands where treasure chests are buried? Some ships are large, but many brave souls sail into the unknown in dinghies and there are rare ones who drift about without a care, but most feel vulnerable, so form squadrons or even flotillas. Indeed, it is a mighty metaphor.

There is much to contemplate in the mighty metaphor and though questions are many sure answers are few. So, it is wisdom to acknowledge our ignorance as being so much greater than our proud knowledge. Not to worry, no matter what, we must sail on and -

Dance the air with the falling leaves,
The fruitful earth, its many sheaves.
Let the merry movements weave,
About the arcane void
Where our hearts beat.
Chant to the beat of the cosmic drum,
While topsy atoms spin and hum,
Rhythms, movements all succumb,
To the silent space
Where our hearts beat.
Move with the sea and the rollicking waves,
Sweeps of sand they pound and lave,
Dirge the gloom of a sea weed cave,
Down to the joy-springs
Where our hearts beat.

❧

"Keep your raft, says Ramprasad,
Afloat on the sea of life,
Drifting up with the floodtide,
Drifting down with the ebb.

EVOLUTION WITH A CAPITAL E AND UNNATURAL SELECTION

By astute observation and much experience Wallace and Darwin discovered a process Darwin called Natural Selection. As with so many scientific theories it was so enthusiastically adopted that it either hid or ignored other facts or issues, leaving them unanswered or unasked. There are many. Natural selection cannot account for why some creatures became birds so long ago but natural selection is assumed. Nor can evolutionary theory explain how they managed to make wings out of arms and hands.

One thing is sure; it must have taken a long time to develop and survival must have been compromised in the interim. How is it possible for some creatures to radically modify a body part to achieve a desire or advantage? There is one creature in Madagascar that has managed to elongate a digit to an extreme length in order to access a preferred food. The ability for a creature to will such a change could be called *psychomorphism.* It functions too, when a person causes changes in the brain and nervous system in order to master a discipline or alter their behavior under the influence of religion or in an attempt to gain elevated levels of consciousness as does the yogi.

Evolutionary theories don't explain how some plants mimic the pheromones of a species of insects, as well as structures, that fool a male of the species to attempt to mate with it, fathering nothing but cross pollination. The human desire to know is also an urge and ability free of natural selection.

Originally Darwin's concept of 'the survival of the fittest' was nothing like it is now thought to mean for the idea has been ruthlessly exploited by the strong, philosophers, sociologists and politicians to further their aims. It really means survival of the *best adapted* and that may be through generations of psychomorphism. Thought of as strength and power it is not so as far as evolution is concerned for dinosaurs were big and strong and aggressive but didn't survive while some small weak animals survived to further life's experiments with evolution.

In the vast amount of Sanskrit literature there may be some revelations concerning evolution, but from my limited reading I know of only one. It is from Patanjali's Yoga Sutras and reads: *Evolution is by the infilling of nature.* Reading this always give me the feeling of a vast everlasting reservoir of potentials existing in a hidden cloud of eternity waiting to manifest in the temporal world of nature. The notion then follows of every evolutionary potential being here now in its fullness, so the ultimate end of the evolutionary process is actually within its emerging forms, no matter how primitive. In this context evolution is nature's struggle to bring these potentials into actuality through the torturous meanderings of time.

And this, in turn, provokes the ideas of drama, game and aesthetics for the fossil record shows that evolution has a direction.

Evidently not a blind force then, in Vedantic terms?

Darwinian evolution is seen as confuting creationism but as Vedanta is synthetic and all-encompassing it sees the conflict as unnecessary. It is not a matter of either/or but of and/and – which is typical of the Vedanta philosophy. Also, its ideas of creation are vastly different from the biblical version. There is no mighty bloke sitting in an antiseptic heaven manufacturing everything down here on earth, as depicted by Michelangelo. As with science, creation is seen as transformational; that is, a development from a simple beginning to complexity.

In one school of Vedanta creation starts from primordial energy (*prakriti*) then from a trinity of three creative 'strings' called *gunas, through* to five basic energies ultimately manifesting as mind, the senses and the elements of earth. Another school sees creation as apparitional - well thought out but as difficult to comprehend as quantum mechanics. Such a brief description is a travesty but cannot be avoided in a short essay.

Further, creation is cyclic, without a beginning or end. The great Hindu sage Kanada (pre 500 BC) developed concepts of time scales and relativity that put the age of this cosmos at 4,300,560,000 years called a day of creation. This figure is based on the length of the solar year and a multiple of pi (the ratio of the circumference to the diameter of a circle). The duration of the whole universe is 314,159,000,000,000 years. Whether accurate or not, the intellectual feat is staggering. Their great astronomer Arya Bhata (476 AD) calculated the circumference of the earth and the law of gravitation and knew the solar system to be heliocentric. This solar system orbits another far distant sun causing seasons of evolutionary change as the progress of our planet causes the seasons. How different to European ideas of the same periods!

This is the final stanza from a creation hymn from the ancient Rig Veda:

He from whom all this great creation sprang,
Whether His will created or was mute,
The most High Seer in the highest heaven,
He knows it – or perchance even He knows not.

Vedanta cosmology has been shown to accord with the concepts of nuclear physics but is capable of going beyond it, for nuclear physics cannot divine the cause of hydrogen, energy or inertia for they existed prior to transformational creation described by physics. At present it seems to be an impasse. Darwinism is focused only on the physical changes and theoretical causes. But evolution also involves changes in consciousness with much greater consequences. The British biologist Sir Julian Huxley wrote in 'Evolution after Darwin' published in 1959:

> *Man's evolution is not biological but psychosocial: it operates by the mechanism of cultural tradition...Accordingly, major steps in the human phase of evolution are achieved by break-throughs to new dominant patterns of mental organization, of knowledge, ideas, and beliefs...*

And here the Vedanta sails evolution into vaster oceans.

The sage Shankara wrote that there were three great boons possible in life – a human incarnation, the desire for freedom and the guidance of a Guru.

It suggests that we individuals were present at the beginning of life and have evolved from primitive forms to other species to finally become human.

The implications imply an evolution in consciousness from the gross animal awareness to the primitive human to the supreme animal and all that that involves in terms of the brain and civilization, ethics, art, literature, religion, philosophy, politics and so on. The implications are wonderful to contemplate.

It must be so that some individuals are human for the first time while others have been human for thousands of years. The ramifications of this are profound. But having achieved human status is not the end. Having experienced lower life forms and achieving human birth, the individual must experience many human births as its consciousness and understanding expands.

Having evolved upwards over millennia to a person with amazing faculties of comprehension, the individual becomes engrossed in the play of egocentric life until it dawns that the play is not all and involves too much conflict and suffering. The significance of life lies beyond the world. It is within consciousness itself.

Having reached this point of understanding, spiritual evolution then begins. The majority of people live life in a cloud of unknowing. Those who live evolving consciously are few. Those who do, ultimately become saints or sages, free of evolution but not yet of residual karma. The sage Shankara describes the end point of human evolution in this way:

> There is a continuous consciousness of the unity of Atman (the soul) with Brahman (the absolute). There is no longer any identification of the Atman with its coverings. All sense of duality is obliterated. There is only pure, unified consciousness. The person who is well established in this consciousness is said to be illumined. Their bliss is unending; they almost forget this world of appearances. Even though the mind is dissolved in Brahman, they are fully awake, but free from the ignorance of waking life. Fully conscious, they are free from any craving. Such a person is free even in this life. For them, the sorrows of this world are over. Though they possess a finite body they remain united with the infinite. They know no anxiety...

Individuality and the acts done in these many comings and goings involve other, subtler laws of life. Just as natural selection is regarded as a law of evolution so are the laws of karma and reincarnation but are of greater significance seeing that they involve the daily life of us all.

Life presents many facts that are impossible to fathom if karma and reincarnation is not taken as a hypothesis, for like gravity or thermodynamics they are part of the laws of life, though being subtle are not open to experimental proof; however, they can be inferred by astute observation and deep contemplation.

One challenging hitherto unaccounted-for fact is the birth of prodigies who possess knowledge or abilities not acquired in this life. The other is the unfortunate ones born severely disadvantaged mentally or physically. *(In this as in other matters, when science ascribes a cause to such things it might be a scientific fact, but it is also a philosophical error, for the assumed cause is in fact, an agent of karma.)*

There are also huge gaps in the theory of evolution apart from those in the fossil record. Biological science is full of unknowns and suppositions made with little evidence and covered by such terms as 'chance variations', 'sporadic changes' or 'spontaneous mutations' and the like. Such terms are in fact an admission of ignorance. Although scientists would be unlikely to agree, the unknowns can be accounted for by the teachings of Vedanta.

According to the sages, the modern idea of everything being controlled solely by genetics or heredity is untenable. Vedanta agrees that heredity and environment are factors in the development of an individual, but that the problems caused by regarding them as the only factors are solved by the doctrines of karma and reincarnation. Heredity factors are then not limited to the parents but are also due to the influences carried over from an incarnating individual's past life. Not only that, the individuals' environment as well as the reactions they take to it are also the result of karmic influence.

Until science can account for sane children born to morons, geniuses born to mediocre parents, or how one child amongst six siblings is brilliant and the others dull and explain idiot savants and other such anomalies they must admit their limitations. Until psychologists can explain how some with traumatic pasts are strong and well balanced, and those who know only security and ease are neurotic, unbalanced and weak, they too, should acknowledge the need for an all-encompassing teaching that can resolve all these issues.

Evolution from animal to human and reincarnation and karma also explains why there is such inequality in intelligence, opportunity and ability in normal births. From another point of view it is a fact that at the birth of every creature consciousness reincarnates. That is a data of observation and cannot be denied.

There is also evidence of personal identity surviving death from people who remember past lives that investigation proved to be so. The weakness is that such claims are always subject to controversy, though it is common for people to get intimations of past births or strong, unaccountable déjà vu – wondered at but often not mentioned to others. I have evidence of such in my own life.

An afterlife is not a subject an ordinary person is not qualified to consider or understand for they are our ordinary experiences taken a cycle up.

This is the reasoning:

The microcosm reflects the macrocosm. The first law of thermodynamics states that energy cannot be created or destroyed and as we are various forms of energy our pattern of energy cannot be destroyed though subject to radical transformation. Just as the few chemical constituents of a body are recycled, so too are the constituents of the soul as a person (*jiva* in Sanskrit) though it involves a transition to another plane of being.

As daily cycles go, it is our common experience that time is spent awake in which we know the external world and internal states. Growing tired we then sleep deeply, a state in which there is no consciousness of a body or an external world, or an internal state. Sometimes we dream in which case the awareness of exclusively internal states occurs. The images we see then are created out of our own consciousness from memories of the external experiences and observed by the witnessing soul. We then wake to earthly experience again. In this way, the twenty-four-hour cycle of human experience mirrors the great cycle of death and rebirth, for in a relative sense we have lived, died, existed in a reality that has no content, experienced only internal images while comatose in dream and came back to waking life again. In this way being born, living in a body, dying, existing without one and then becoming embodied again is simply the ordinary daily experience on a greater cycle on a larger time scale. A sleeping person is often said to be 'dead to the world'. When the bio-energies (*pranas*) leave the body it is dead; the bodies few chemicals and the pranas along with mind-stuff (*chitta)* is recycled; the *jiva* reduced to a spark of awareness is then on another plane of being. The soul, according to the level of awareness while alive, experiences little or nothing, or the joy of pure uncontaminated consciousness (call it heaven) or the images of a dream. If the images are pleasant we could be said to be in a sort of heaven, if bad, in a sort of hell. As in life the dreams are all from within our own consciousness

The spiritually evolved go to higher planes and may not need to be reincarnated back to this one. Those of evil tendencies cannot enjoy the freedom of not having a body and are limited to lower planes of existence and suffer because they cannot experience the satisfactions of gross desires that require a physical body to experience. Very frustrating. (Call it purgatory). Some become poltergeists and ghosts and may be reborn in bodies that can express only lower levels of consciousness. They have to start all over again like a player of snakes and ladders who loses the throw and must go back to square one.

So according to Vedanta evolution is constant for those beings with a human body have reached the epitome of animal evolution but have began another phase; their further development to ultimate freedom from evolutionary imperatives is inevitable over the millennia to come.

This is karma with a capital K and evolution with a capital E.

Darwin was reticent in publishing *On the Origin of Species,* not so much because he feared conflict with the Church or the disapproval of his wife, a devout Christian, but that it pulled the rug out from under the prevailing scientific dogmas of the age that were based upon the notion that the universe was a giant machine whose laws and life forms were fixed from the beginning. The observations of Wallace and Darwin did much to renovate these old notions. It could be said that Darwin did for biology what the early nuclear physicists did for physics as in both cases their theories caused a revolution in these disciplines. The ideas extolled in Vedanta philosophy have done the same for nuclear physics and may one day do the same for biology and evolutionary theory – but I doubt it.

> *The world has been evolved, not created: it has arisen little by little from a small beginning and has increased through the activity of the elemental forces embodied in itself and so has grown rather than come into being at an almighty word. What a sublime idea of the infinite might of the great Architect, the Cause of all causes, the Father of all fathers. For if we would compare the Infinite it would surely require a greater Infinite to cause the causes of effects than to produce the effects themselves.*
>
> Erasmus Darwin 1731-1802

According the Vedanta it is possible that he became reincarnated in 1809 as his great grandchild Charles (1809 – 1882) in order to further his work...

SHIVA AND SCIENCE

Few people realize the debt science and mathematics owe to Hindu culture. The idea of zero was the invention of a Hindu sage and its use unshackled mathematics. Its sign is a symbol for infinity (0). Its use freed mathematics from the cumbersome, space consuming way of writing numbers, such as the Roman. The next step was then possible, the use of the zero as a moving dot – in other words, the decimal point. Philosophically the eternity of the circle represents the infinite. It is the genius of the Hindu spirit to make a tenet of religious philosophy a practical principle of mathematics.

Many centuries ago the great Hindu sage Kanada (pre 500 BC) developed concepts of time scales and relativity that put the age of this cosmos at 4,300,560,000 years called a day of creation. This figure is based on the length of the solar year and a multiple of pi (the ratio of the circumference to the diameter of a circle) The duration of the whole universe is 314,159,000,000,000 years. Whether accurate or not, the intellectual feat is staggering. Their great astronomer Arya Bhata (476 AD) calculated the circumference of the earth and the law of gravitation and knew the solar system to be heliocentric.

The extent of the interaction between ancient cultures is not appreciated by most people, so the fact of India's contribution to world knowledge is unknown. Two thousand five hundred years ago Indian Universities in Taxila and Nalanda led the world in science, arts and philosophy and attracted students from as far away as Greece, Korea, Persia and China. Many of the basic concepts of modern day science were known.

Two events occurred in the 1890's to rectify the misconceptions: one in America, the other in Europe. The Hindu monk, Swami Vivekananda, shook America with the truth, lecturing throughout the States. His impact upon western culture is not capable of evaluation, but his most rewarding exchanges were between professors at universities and scientists such as Tesla and Edison. In Europe, Hindu philosophical works such as the Upanishads and Bhagavad Gita were becoming known. Schopenhauer, Maeterlinck and others made mention of their debt, as did Edison, Emerson, Thoreau and later, the physicists Bohr, Oppenheimer, Heisenberg and others. The result of this introduction of Hindu philosophy and culture produced the phenomena known as the New Age. It could also be said that a New Age began with the discoveries of nuclear physics which has produced a new way of thinking. The New Age is due to both these scientific and spiritual advents.

The old paradigms were that the universe was a vast machine run on everlasting rules of engineering or laws of nature, that matter was a dead stuff informed and motivated by forces separate from it, and to be universally workable, these forces must be the same at all times and in all places. Hence matter and energy, mind and matter, God and man etc were utterly different in nature.

This being the fundamental notion, the question to be answered was how one affected, or acted upon the other. This was the concern of the great physicist Newton from whom we inherit the notion of the billiard-ball structure of atoms and the mechanistic ideas of nature. Modern atomic physicists cannot make much use of these concepts, for the experimental data demand completely new ideas. The expression of the new ideas sounds similar to the writings of oriental cultures and some scientific theories begin to sound like Asian philosophy. This does not mean they are equivalent, however.

Though the old mechanical ideas of physics are still accurate enough within their frames of reference, they are too limited to encompass the new reality revealed by the mysteries of relativity and quantum theory. They seem to require an existential leap beyond common sense. It is this leap demanded by the new data that appeals to the followers of Vedanta, Taoist and Buddhist philosophy. This leap took atomic scientists from a dualistic worldview to a more unitive understanding in contrast with the dualistic/mechanistic paradigms then in vogue. The leap caused the great physicists of last century to become mystics to one extent or the other as their writings show.

The following quote has some similarities to Vedantic ideas

'A human being is part of the whole called by us the 'Universe', a part limited in time and space. He experiences himself, his thoughts and feelings, as something separate from the rest – a kind of optical delusion of his consciousness. This delusion is a kind of prison for us, restricting us to our personal desires and to affections for a few persons nearest to us. Our task must be to free ourselves from this prison by widening our circle of compassion to embrace all living creatures and the whole of nature in its beauty. Nobody is able to achieve this completely, but the striving for this achievement is in itself a part of the liberation and a foundation for inner security '. Albert Einstein, *The New York Post,* 28 November 1972.

Advaita Vedanta is a non-dualistic philosophy so all-encompassing that it does not deny dualistic philosophies but integrates them into a higher understanding. It regards dualistic religions and philosophies as being necessary steps to a unified knowledge, just as the 'old science' has been to the startling new science of quantum theory. In a similar fashion quantum physics grew out of Newton's physics and the one really significant difference between them according to Sir Arthur Eddington, is that

Quantum physics has been forced to acknowledge that it does not deal with ultimate reality. The Advaitic view is that duality is the temporal world experience projected by the mind upon an eternal non-dual, ultimate reality. Theories of science are heading in this direction if Einstein's 'unified field' is the ultimate reality. So, the apparent duality is based upon a non-dual reality. This is the fundamental principle of the ancient Vedanta.

When opposites are regarded as absolute and duality rules, knowledge is divided into apparently conflicting principles. How does mind relate to matter? Matter to energy? Man to nature? God to man? And so on. In the light of Vedanta, Western philosophy and science have struggled to bridge gaps that don't really exist; to unify parts of a single body and reconcile differences between opposites that are only apparent. This mental attitude was the main block to understanding the strange things that arose from the experiments of atomic physics. The wiser Orientals, imbued with the realization that what appears to be in opposition, is in reality, complementary, had no such need.

So it was that the old attitudes had to give way to a theory that unified the conflicts and all the observed data – a task so difficult that it seems it may never be fully worked out, though much has been achieved by the great physicists of last century. Their theories include such ideas as the backward flow of time, the non-existence of discrete particles and the equivalence of such bodies to the space in which they seem to exist, indeterminacy, noncausality, multiple dimensions and so on. (Such notions are contrary to common sense, fact quantum theories share with some doctrines of spiritual philosophy and one major reason why they can sound so alike when expressed in ordinary language).

Albert Einstein has written: 'We may therefore regard matter as being constituted by the region of space in which the field is extremely intense...there is no place in this new kind of physics for both the field and matter, for the field is the only reality.'

Again: 'The field exists always and everywhere; it can never be removed. It is the carrier of all material phenomena...It is the void out of which the proton creates the pimesons. Being and fading of particles are merely forms of the motion of the field'

This is a far cry from Newtonian billiard balls of basic stuff being pushed around by electromagnetic forces. It means that the total, inconceivable power and energy of the field is 'locked' into what appears to our senses to be material bodies. This was first theoretically demonstrated by Einstein's famous equation E= MC 2. It is interesting to learn how he arrived at it.

In 1905 Einstein wrote a paper using electromagnetic equations to show that anybody which takes in an amount of energy of any sort, (or releases it) gains (or loses) an amount of mass. This may be infinitesimal. If a 100-watt electric light bulb emitted energy as light for 100 years, the loss of its total mass would be less than a millionth of an ounce. Two years later it dawned upon him that if energy had mass then mass must have energy. It took 25 years for the equation to be confirmed, for to do so required technological and experimental breakthroughs. The tragedy is that this inspiring truth gave birth to the atomic bomb and Hiroshima.

What does it mean, this E=MC2? E, (the energy contained in a particle) is equal to the particle's mass (M) times the square of the speed of light (C2). Expressed in words it means that one gram of matter converted to energy becomes 900 billion billion ergs.

Imagine the consequences of such a realization! Every speck of matter, every speck of earth, every pebble, every flower petal, so solid or so soft, holds a reservoir of prodigious energy. While physics might postulate such a theory, only the trained mystic can experience it as a reality – and this is the vital difference between them. This scientific truth has been expressed in Hindu philosophy for thousands of years.

Enter Shiva

A quality of energy (called prana in Hindu philosophy) is change and movement, epitomized by the Hindu God Shiva in His aspect of Natarajan, the cosmic dancer. Is this another mythological image, a piece of fanciful sculpture? It may well be all things. Like beautiful scientific ideas it is elegant and aesthetically satisfying, for it is art, poetry and science.

Ananda Coomaraswami, writing about Natarajan: 'He rising from his rapture and dancing sent through inert matter, pulsating waves of awakening sound and lo! Matter also dances! Appearing as a glory round about him. Dancing, he sustains its manifold phenomena. In the fullness of time, still dancing, he destroys all forms and names by fire and gives new rest. This is poetry, but nonetheless, science.'

Solid matter hides a chaos of movement. The wild pattern of particles coming and going, appearing and disappearing, whose traces can be photographed in a bubble chamber shows this pulsating dance of creation and destruction. Like an equation, the beautiful image of the dancing Shiva develops a theme – the upper right hand holds a drum, indicating the patterns of rhythmic change and the primordial sound of creation verbally expressed in the mantra OM. The upper left holds a tongue of flame, the symbol of converting matter into prana – the element of destruction. He is encircled by flames, a symbol of energy. The dance itself is the conversion of prana into matter. The dynamic tension between the hands indicates the balance of forces of creation and destruction. The second right hand is raised in a gesture, which says, 'Do not fear, for while ever I dance all creatures will exist. When I cease dancing all creatures will return to Me.'

The lower left hand points to the demigod Pralaya or oblivion, which at once symbolizes the great night of creation or in – breathing when the universe is utterly non-existent - or the death of personal ignorance when transcendental knowledge dawns.

For either, Shiva must stop dancing for Pralaya to rise. The image means that rhythmic motion supports the universe and when it stops not even one speck of dust could remain. On the personal level, it means that when the dance of thoughts and dualistic tensions cease, one is free in transcendental union with Shiva. The Hindu scriptures put it this way: 'When a man is in the embrace of a loving wife he knows nothing within or without, so a person when in the embrace of the intelligent spirit, knows nothing within or without'...'Where there is duality, there one sees another, smells another, tastes another, but where everything has become one's own Self, then whereby and whom could one see or smell, or taste?'

Is this void and non-dual state the background of personal consciousness? Science could not affirm such a thing, but Shiva is depicted as human, for of all animals the human being is the most conscious and intelligent. The anthropomorphic image is closer to the truth than an equation could ever be, for prana is intelligent. Is Shiva, the cosmic dancer, moving in the universal void? Is the unified field of physics synonymous with the Buddhists' emptiness or the Hindus' Pralaya and is Shiva a way of explaining the dance of matter revealed by the wild comings and goings of who knows what recorded by the experiments of nuclear science? It is easy to see parallels and exploring them is an interesting pastime as legitimate as any other, though when a similarity is taken as identical proof error creeps in. The differences are great and are probably not reconcilable. The major conflicts involve the phenomena of consciousness, the concept of God and the relationship of humans to the creator. In the main, when science does not flatly deny their existence, it denies their importance. Mysticism is based upon them and denies the importance of science as a means to realization. One is theoretical, the other experiential. One is capable of being really understood only by a few highly trained physicists, but profound mystical ideas are available to all.

This is something of great significance that older civilizations, specifically the Hindu, accomplished. *Because of this sort of mythology cosmic truths were made accessible to all, no matter how educated or ignorant, for mythology talks in the hidden language of the unconscious, not the abstractions of mathematics, understood only by a privileged few.* The inability of science to illuminate the deep issues of life is absolute for reasons the great physicists are adamant in affirming as we shall see. Astrophysics reveals another parallel, having accepted the big bang theory of cosmic origin, and the concomitant of the expanding universe. This is the subject of many Hindu writings. The Vishnu Purana explains the dance of creation as a movement of expansion and contraction in rhythmic cycles of vast time, with one cycle of alternate creation and dissolution spanning 369.95616 trillion human years. Is it a coincidence that the word 'Brahman', who is the Absolute beyond the trinity of the Gods of creation, preservation and destruction comes from the Sanskrit root 'Brih', to expand?

The Zen parallels

The closest verbal parallels between concepts of nuclear physics and Asian worldviews exist in Taoist and Zen texts. Compare the following statement of D.T Suzuki with the one following by Einstein.

'There are no divisions such as past, present and future, for they have contracted into a single moment where life quivers in its true sense...the past and the future are rolled up in this present moment of illumination.' And from Einstein:

'For us believing physicists the distinction between past present and future is only an illusion...'

In the words of his friend Robert Oppenheimer:

'If we ask for instance whether the position of the electron remains the same, we must say 'no', if we ask if the electron's position changes with time, we must say 'no'. If we ask whether the electron is at rest we must say 'no'. If we ask if it is in motion, we must say 'no'.

Sounds very much like this verse from the Hindu Upanishads -

'It moves, it moves not. It is far, it is near, It is within all this, It is outside all this. It is not being or becoming, it is neither existence nor non existence, neither this nor that.'

In other words, the fundamental reality is non-dual, like the Tao of Zen and the unified field of physics, though one is a theory and the other a spiritual realization. Reading of both, it is easy to believe that they refer to the same things. The similarity is most striking in the comparison between the physicists' time/space vacuum and the Buddhists void and the Zen Tao.

The next two quotations could be expected to come from a modern scientific treatise. The first however is from the works of Lama Govinda:

'The relationship of form and emptiness cannot be conceived as a state of mutually exclusive opposites, but only as two aspects of the same reality which co-exist and are in mutual co-operation'.

And from an ancient Sutra, 'Form is emptiness, emptiness is indeed form'

Quantum field theory posits such a vacuum or field in which all the atomic events take place. This is not a stagnant vacuum but rather a dynamic one, for the events that take place are a form of the field, and the field a form of the events. This is an exact parallel to the dynamic void of Taoist and Zen writings. The void is not a dead nothing, but an absolute potential, for it gives birth to all possible forms and movements.

Chang Tsai said it perfectly, using the Zen term 'Chi', which literally means, 'vapour' but is best thought of as cosmic energy.

'The great void cannot but consist of chi; this chi cannot but condense to form all things and these things cannot but disperse so as to form once more the great void...When one knows that the great void is full of chi one knows there is no such thing as emptiness.'

It is possible that the future ideas of high-energy physics may reveal something of the mystery of consciousness, a subject that it has steered away from until recently. There is a growing concern amongst researchers that to observe an experiment is to condition the results, and that consciousness, along with all other aspects of nature, is necessary for the consistency of the whole. Not only that, but nature seems to answer our questions according to the way we ask it. If you ask an electron or light, a particle question it will give a particle answer; if asked as a wave it answers as a wave. This strangeness caused the great physicist Werner Heisenberg to write:

'Natural science does not simply describe and explain nature; it is part of the interplay between matter and ourselves.'

In an interview published in the *Observer* in 1931 Max Planck said:

'I regard consciousness as fundamental. I regard matter as a derivative from consciousness. We cannot get behind consciousness. Everything that we talk about, everything that we postulate as existing requires consciousness.'

Considering consciousness as part of the fundamental reality of the universe, Hindu and Chinese sages have gone about as far as thought and realization can go. To them, all forms of life share some degree of the same basic consciousness, being part of an inseparable whole. Further, the Hindu Vedanta philosophers declare consciousness to be the ultimate reality. It is called intelligence, existence and bliss absolute, though it is understood that the absolute in itself can possess no parts. The Vedanta philosophy goes even further, for it teaches that individual identity has it roots in Brahman, the absolute intelligence, existence and bliss. It places the intuition of 'I am' at the beginning of all manifestation, reversing the dictum of Descartian philosophy, 'I think, therefore I am 'with 'I am, therefore I think'.

It is this sense of being which must precede the perception of all phenomena. It is the Ultimate playing in the worlds of creation; none other than God manifesting His magic, hidden in the illusions of time, space and causation. The divine then appears, not as a stern ruler directing all from on high, but the nature of things, informing all life from within. This is a constant theme in Hindu scripture:

> 'He who, dwelling in all things yet is other than all things,
> Who all things do not know, but who controls all things from within,
> He is your spirit, the inner controller, the immortal'

It should be acknowledged that physics could not reveal such things. There are two reasons for this. The most salient fact is that Quantum Physics is not a reading of reality. Sir James Jeans emphasized this when he wrote in his book *Physics and Philosophy*: 'our studies can never put us into contact with reality; we can never penetrate beyond the impressions that reality implants in our minds.'

Physics is limited to highly abstract differential equations – a shadow world of symbols analysing a shadow world of markings on a photographic plate – as the greatest of the nuclear physicists have been the first to point out.

The physicist and the mystic share the same difficulty when they attempt to express their understanding in ordinary language. Their statements may appear to be ambiguous, paradoxical, and obscure to common sense. This is the main reason why they often sound so similar. It is a fact of great significance that all the great physicists have warned against attempting to apply theories of physics to human life. Discussing this with Max Planck, Einstein said "The present fashion of applying the axioms of physical science to human life is not only entirely a mistake but has also something reprehensible in it." - *The more so when the notions are selected with bias in order to support a belief system.*

Werner Heisenberg was even more to the point when he wrote, 'Many modern creeds which claim that they are in fact, not dealing with acts of faith, but are based on scientific knowledge, contain inner conflicts and rest on self-deception.'

The last word on the implausibility of applying scientific principles to common life goes to the great physicist Sir Arthur Eddington who described the impasse in his book 'The Nature of the Physical World' published in 1929.

'The materialist who is convinced that all phenomena arise from electrons and quanta and the like, controlled by mathematical formulae, must presumably hold the belief that his wife is a rather elaborate differential equation, but he is probably tactful enough not to obtrude this opinion into his domestic life. If this kind of scientific dissection is felt to be inadequate and irrelevant in ordinary personal relationships, it is surely out of place in the most personal relationship of all – that of the human soul to a divine spirit. '

To illustrate the nonsensical result of looking at life in the concepts of science he writes:

'I am standing on the threshold about to enter a room. It is a complicated business. In the first place I must shove against an atmospheric pressure with a force of fourteen pounds per square inch of my body. I must make sure of landing on a plank travelling at twenty miles a second round the sun. – a fraction of a second too early or too late and the plank would be miles away. I must do this while hanging from a round planet head outward into space and with a wind of ether blowing at no one knows at how many miles a second through every interstice of my body. The plank has no solidarity of substance. To step on it is like stepping on a swarm of flies. Shall I not slip through? No, if I make the gesture a fly hits me and gives a boost up again. I fall again and am knocked upwards by another fly and so on. I may hope that the net result will be that I remain about steady, but if, unfortunately I should slip through the floor or be boosted violently up to the ceiling, the occurrence would be, not a violation of the laws of Nature, but a rare coincidence. These are some of the minor difficulties... It is necessary to determine in which direction the entropy of the world is increasing in order to make sure that my entrance is not an exit. Verily, it is easier for a camel to pass through the eye of a needle than for a scientific man to pass through a door...'

A truth not considered by New Age enthusiasts who build their edifice of belief upon the theories of theoretical physics is that they are building their house on quicksand, for the only sure thing is that these theories will undergo radical change. The ideas taken as supporting New Age spiritualism are likely to join the thousands of other ideas in the cemetery of science's dead and buried theories.

Whatever happens, Shiva will continue dancing; on his face, an enigmatic smile.

THE GREY BETWEEN BLACK AND WHITE

A few miles south of Urunga, a small town on the coast, there is a worn-down headland called Hungry Head. Local law has it that it was given this name way back, when the few people who lived in Urunga used it as a lookout to see if the supply ship bringing food and booze was coming. It is also supposed to be the site of the river mouth long ago, so what was once riverbed is now a patch of littoral rainforest festooned with creepers and vines. Up on the headland there are huge old paperbark trees gnarled as gnomes, leaning away from the sea winds, some twisted branches blown horizontal high above the native violets and grasses. From the grassy headland one can see as far north as Coff's Harbour and as far south as Smoky Cape. High above the beach behind the tangle of literal rainforest the land has been cleared of the blaidy grass and bracken undergrowth and looks like a park timbered with bloodwood, brush box and Banksia. It is a most pleasant place.

Wandering there this morning I found something unusual. It was a mound about 1.5 metres long and 60cm wide with large smooth river stones visible through the sandy soil. The stones don't belong there and must have been brought from up river many kilometres away. The shape, size and location suggest that it is the remnants of an aboriginal oven. Not far away, a bloodwood has had its bark removed at about my shoulder height, in the shape of a small shield or Coolamon. Question: who but an aboriginal would have bothered to do this and moreover, when? Taking a guess at the age of the tree, slow-growing in poor soil, at about one hundred years, it must have been a seedling sometime in the 19th century. The area was settled by Europeans in the late 1840's.

Since early boyhood I have been mindful of the presence and absence of the original inhabitants of Australia. Somewhere, somehow, I had found a book illustrating aboriginal art and designs taken from tree and rock carvings and cave and body paintings or those on shields or sacred tcheringa stones. Often I studied it, responding to it in a strange way. I was happy to be given an ashtray by David and Hermia Boyd years later, when they had a pottery in Neutral Bay. It was covered in the same aboriginal depictions of wildlife I recognized from my book. This was about 1945. Maybe it was the first time aborigine motifs were used on household items.

French's Forest was at my doorstep and that was where I spent most of my boyhood. I would often find a place that hid secrets I knew were theirs. I found many of their carvings but always longed to find a boomerang or a stone axe. Hopefully I have dug in the soil of caves or sandstone overhangs but have found nothing. I found that getting reliable information about the original inhabitants was not easy. The details of traditional life were mostly lost, compromised or kept secret in most districts by the 1930's. The suppositions, projections and hearsay of anthropologists or of suburban Aboriginals don't impress me. Mountford's accounts of living with a group in the centre are most authentic and interesting but even so, he was still on the outside. I am now reading a book that purports to explain how the majority of the groups lived in the north but fails to explain the trivial details that constitute most of our life – what were the practices of hygiene, especially for women? Did they keep something over to eat for breakfast? What were the social laws governing interactions and hygiene when large numbers met for corroborees? What were the sexual practices and morals? Did they wash regularly or not at all? Did they care for their teeth? Did they wash or wipe their anus or neither? Were areas around a camp set aside for sex or defecation and were the faeces buried? How did they carry water? (I asked this question of an Aboriginal ranger at Uluru after being told that tribes came from distant places to Uluru. He said it was probably in a Coolamon, but I doubt it. After a day walking carrying it on a hip I think there would be little water left.) Did they sleep on the ground in pouring rain and what were the methods of staying warm while sleeping at zero temperatures? The book contains photos, supposedly of traditional life but they were taken about 1890. Some of the men have hair and moustaches that have been trimmed or cut and wear strips of cloth to hide the offending genitals. One wears an unlikely mess of trailing furs with the fur on the outside, though it was usually worn on the inside. Fair dinkum? I don't think so.

The book also refers to medicines being made by boiling water, though the aborigines had no containers sufficient for this purpose and there are accounts by early explorers of the startling effects on them when they saw water boiling for the first time. The many whites who lived with them as tribal members gave no secrets away when they finally joined their own people. I give up. It seems it is too late to search for infallible, authentic facts. There are however, some facts to balance the current obsession with the historical facts of murder and massacres.

The truth is that there were atrocities and massacres on both sides. It was an undeclared war without a Geneva Convention. But as always, there is another side to the gruesome history.

One Narcisse Pellatier was a cabin boy on a French ship that got wrecked on the coast of north Queensland in 1858. He lived with the natives for 17 years until taken by force back to 'civilization'. He returned to Europe but after many years, went back to his tribe and was never seen again. The most interesting and significant case was the discovery of a wild white boy and his mother who had been shipwrecked in the 1860's. They were found by a police party from Derby in the 1890's. The finding was reported to Governor Broome via the new overland telegraph. The Governor sent his welcome to them and requested them to join the police and be escorted back to civilization. The old woman thanked him in return but added that they were quite happy and felt no compulsion to do so. They too, were never seen again. William Buckley was a convict who joined the tribe in the Melbourne area and lived with them for 30 years, was found and pardoned but became morose and died after a few years. The twin culture shocks he experienced would have been very unsettling.

The extent of the arrogance of the 'civilized' is beyond belief. Taking the high moral ground and well schooled in duplicity by society, the language and seeking wealth through living lives of individual competitiveness, the traditional communalism and reciprocity of the aborigines appeared as childlike and primitive. Though it is becoming more appreciated, our pervasive conditioning prevents us from knowing the deep significance of their culture. Much of their language has been lost or distorted; and as language is the carrier of culture, so the original culture has been lost and distorted – except for a few elders in limited and isolated areas, who still keep their secrets. It is difficult for us to realize that their stories, myths and rituals express truths rational expressions cannot.

The growing awareness of the horrors inflicted upon a whole race of people by overrunning their lands, denigrating them and attempting to destroy their culture is taking a few pathetic forms, from saying sorry to acknowledging that certain areas were once inhabited by specific tribes. Each morning when Joe O'Brian hosts the morning news on the ABC, he acknowledges that it comes from the lands of the Cadigal people. Though this admission might help ease a guilty conscience, it must be sorrowing for the few Cadigals still on their ancestral territory; it is no longer Cadigal country but the brick, cement and asphalt country of the usurping people. It is ironically fitting that many new Australians come from counties that were once the victims of similar take-overs.

We have focused so much attention of late on the violent and negative interaction of the two cultures that the other truth is neglected. Many of the early squatters had good reciprocal relations with the local tribes and many tribesmen became close friends and helpers as the history of the Duracks in southwest Queensland and many others, shows. Of such a one, Patrick Durack said decades later that one of the tribesmen was the best friend he ever had. It is only fair to acknowledge that it would have been impossible for us to pioneer this country without their help. Some escapees from the prison settlement in Brisbane wandered about the bush for years with help from the locals until death or settlement caught up with them, they were captured or gave themselves up.

Clement Hodgkinson was the Government Surveyor in the Kempsey district who explored the Nambucca and Bellingen River areas in 1841 and 42. He had many aboriginal friends and helpers and was present at many of their corroborees and ceremonies which he both sketched and described. When bitten by a black snake he had the good sense to go to the natives for treatment.

He writes:

'*...they were elaborately painted with white for the occasion, that even their very toes and fingers were carefully and regularly coloured with concentric rings, whilst their hair was drawn up in a close knot and stuck all over with the snowy down of the white cockatoo...in this dance the performers arranged themselves in the form of a semicircle, and grasping the ends of their boomerangs, which are also painted with great minuteness and regularity, they swayed their bodies rapidly from right to left. Each movement of their bodies to and fro was accompanied by a loud hiss whilst a number of other natives similarly painted, beat time with sticks and* *kept up an incessant song. Every now and then the dancers would stop and rush, crowding together into a circle raising their weapons with outstretched arms and joining with frantic energy in the song.'*

Hodgkinson thought that the aborigines were *'too much underrated. In everything requiring the exercise of mechanical ingenuity or dexterity the Australian aborigines are apt scholars. Indeed I think that all endeavours to make them adopt more settled habits will be useless, for what great inducement does the monotonous and toilsome existence of the labouring classes in civilized communities offer to make the savage abandon his independent and carefree life diversified by the exiting occupations off hunting, fighting and dancing.'*

On the 7th of July 1842 the Sydney Morning Herald published a long letter from Edward Ogilvie, a settler on the Clarence River, in support of the aborigines.

> *The only apology I can offer for occupying so large a portion of your valuable space, is, that without entering into the details I could not have obtained the object I had in view, namely, to show the very peaceable disposition and unrevengeful spirit of these people and to convince those who are in the habit of looking upon them as little better than wild beasts, that they are mistaken.*

Amicable relations are also facts of history. The only complaint the Durack family expressed about the local aborigines when they settled in southwest Queensland, was the noise they made every night singing and dancing, blowing didgeridoos and clapping boomerangs together. But they spearheaded the dispossession that took place later.

The advantages of the aboriginal way of life were obvious to others at first contact - the first being Captain Cook. He wrote this in his journal while the Endeavour was being repaired:

'Sunday the 6th 1770...no sort of clothing or ornaments was ever seen by any of us upon any one of them or in or about any of their huts from which I conclude that they never wore any ... they had not so much as touched the things we left in their huts on purpose for them to take away. From what I have said of the Natives of New-Holland they may appear to be the most wretched of people upon Earth, but in reality they are far more happier than we Europeans; being wholly unacquainted not only with the superfluous but the necessary Conveniences so much sort after in Europe, they are happy in not knowing the use of them. They live in a Tranquillity which is not disturbed by the Inequality of Condition: the earth and sea of their own accord furnish them with all things necessary for life, they covet not Magnificent Houses, Household stuff, they live in a warm and fine climate and enjoy a very wholesome Air so that they have very little need of Clothing and this they seem to be very sensible of for many to which we gave Cloth left it carelessly upon the Sea beach and in the woods as they had no manner of use for. In short, they seemed to set no value upon anything we gave them, nor would they part with anything of their own for any article we offer them; this in my opinion argues that they think themselves provided with all the necessaries of life and that they have no superfluities.

Monday 23rd... yesterday I sent some of the people into the Country to gather greens, one of which straggl'd from the rest and met with four of the natives...they suffered him to go away without offering the least insult and perceiving that he did not go right for the ship directed him which way he should go.

❧

Quest

Weary of this web of complex strife,
I long for the free and simple life.
I wistfully gaze on some old thing found,
a spear, a flint, a tool of bone
hidden, for ages, underground,
our forebears used in the age of stone.

The first to come to this austral isle,
show it is not so;
they lived life the same simple way,
Just the other side of yesterday.
Survivors over time's vast span,
they needed nothing more to live,
this austral island's stone age man,
than each other, song and dance,
and whatever nature had to give,
and came by chance.

By power, arrogance and the gun,
so much was lost when so much won;
the lost recourse is here to show,
the wonder of such success;
how much we do not need to know,
and how little to possess.
When our proud world has tumbled
into chaos and decay,
perhaps we may be humbled
to learn from such as they.

PLANTS – EVERYDAY MIRACLES

A few years ago, a friend gave me some lily-like plants that have long thin leaves straight out of the ground. They are blooming now and doing something quite original. The small cream-colored flower of four petals with a purple center pops up out of the top of a long leaf, which then bends down until it touches the ground. Leaves shoot from one side and roots from the other and presto! There comes another one. They have now walked in this way meters from the original plant.

The originality of plant reproduction can be amazing – there is one that has a thin stalk dangling below the flower that ends with an imitation of a species of female beetle. Along comes an unsuspecting male, sees the imitation of its opposite gender, mounts and attempts to fly off with her; up comes the beetle until its back touches the stamen of the flower thus getting covered in pollen - so when it tries it again on another plant fertilization takes place. You might think that this is ingenious enough but wait! There's more! If I didn't know it as a fact, I could scarcely believe it – not only does the plant make a facsimile female beetle but wafts out a scent imitating its inviting pheromones! In the USA there is a very smart cactus that flowers only one night a year but does so on the very night that a nocturnal moth hatches the brood that pollinates it.

It is little known that the biggest living thing is not a whale, but a fungus. It glows underground and can cover an area of many kilometers. They allow trees to communicate with each other. Some fungi are incredible. They can live as separate spores until some mysterious signal makes them seek each other out; they then join to make a multi-celled organism which puts up a penis-like stalk and spurts millions of spores out into the air. They then go their separate ways until the time comes for them to join up again and repeat the performance.

Flowers and plants run the range of size from minute yeasts and spores to flowers smaller than a pinhead to unbelievably large – there is a tropical plant with a single flower that is a meter across. I have walked in the one-tree forest on the banks of the Adyar River on the outskirts of what was once Madras (it is on the in skirts of what is now Chennai.) The forest is actually a fig that covers almost a hectare all on its own, its vast branches supported by adventitious roots.

Plants also run to extremes in lifetimes, some bloom and die in minutes; others live for thousands of years, such as the bristle cone pine. This was considered the oldest living plant until it was discovered that a species of mulga in South Australia outlived even America's gnarled old pines.

Consider then, the strangler fig. How come it only sprouts in the forks of other trees? How is it that it can survive on so little while its adventitious roots slowly grow down into the earth? When established they make interesting shapes. There is one huge old strangler fig in the forest in the border ranges. I have climbed up it *inside* the tree. It is quite hollow; the host tree having rotted away years ago. In the same location are arctic beach thought to be over three thousand years old and a giant red cedar whose huge trunk rises to the canopy without a single branch. The last of its kind, it is just a youngster, estimated to be about a thousand years old.

Plants only invented flowers relatively late in biological time; such a remarkable and successful improvement that the angiosperms populated the whole planet in amazing abundance. There are 25.000 species of orchids alone, some so reliant on specific insects for pollination and the insects on the flower for food, that they could almost be considered as two phases of one creature. The amazing variety of shapes, size, structure and design of flowers beggars the imagination. So much so that I doubt if one possibility has gone unexploited, and no climate they cannot manage to live in. The ability of cacti and succulent to store water in deserts or arid lands; the amazing variety of methods of dispersing seeds or fertilizing them, boggles the mere human brain. There is a grass seed that manages to walk along the ground until it falls into a crevice. To catalogue all the variations would take volumes. Could it be that there exists one person who does not like and enjoy flowers? Of course not – though it has occurred to me that there is something kinky about our cutting the sexual organs of plants off to display them in a vase or make wreaths.

The ability of plants to adapt beggars my comprehension. There are many examples, but that of the carnivorous plants is outstanding. In areas where the soil is deficient in nitrogen, the pitcher plants have evolved pouches with slippery sides that have sticky goo at the base in which there are enzymes that digest any insect that slips into it – thus providing the essential nitrogen. Some have lips like red meat and smell like rotting flesh. Others have senses that close opposing jaws when an insect, lured by the sweet bait enters it. Others trap and digest mice; another provides a meal of a laxative that causes the tree-shrew that eats it to excrete, and the plant dines on that. It's all too much for the human brain. There is a plant in Britain that has learnt to thrive on stone walls. When the time is ripe it sends a long shoot through its leaves out into the sun to flower and get pollinated. That achieved, when the seed sets, the shoot turns around until it touches the stone, then moves about seeking a crevice. Crevice found, the seed awaits rain and the shoot dies.

Many people believe that plants have feelings. I believe that if it is so, it cannot exist without a rudimentary intelligence. As far as I can see, this rudimentary intelligence must infer the presence of a rudimentary psyche as well. This is a beautiful idea and I don't give a damn if it conflicts with current biological dogmas. I like the notion that plants are rudimentary people. On the other hand, maybe we are fully evolved plants.

In the 'Great Forest' Upanishad, which is one of the Hindu scriptures, the sage Yajnavalkya said:

> *'As a mighty tree, so indeed are we. Our hair is the leaves, and our skin is the outer bark. From our skin blood flows and from bark, sap. Therefore, when we are wounded, blood flows as sap from a tree that is injured. Our flesh is its inner bark, and our nerves are its innermost layer. Our bones lay within like the hard wood of a tree and marrow resembles pith. A tree, when it is felled, springs again from its root in a new form; from what root tell me, do we spring forth after we are cut off by death?'*

Plants have at least one rudimentary sense – that of touch.

The Indian biologist who was knighted in 1917 for his research into plant life became famous for the invention of a delicate electronic instrument he called a crescograph. He said to his admirer, the great Yogi Paramhansa Yogananda - as the Swami recorded in his autobiography, 'the telltale charts of my crescograph are evidence for the most skeptical that plants have a sensitive nervous system and a varied emotional life ... other appropriate responses to stimuli are as universal in plants as in animals.' And all this without mention of germinating seeds. A seed may wait in the soil for decades sometimes and when in the mood, can start a process that can be explained. That does not mean that it is any the less inexplicable. Somehow the little seed can make a shoot full of minerals, vitamins and enzymes that were not present before. That is why sprouts are so nutritious.

The ability to search for a support as the creeper on my pergola does and then to cancel the effort when it proves unfruitful, is also a manifestation of a very basic intelligence. Whether or no, it is clever enough to produce these delectable bundles of blooms I like so much.

The other creeper knows how to creep. It needed no help from me. It started from under an azalea bush that grew by a pergola post. The post is square, so I wondered if it would grow straight up, but no, it began to twine around the post of its own accord. A right angle turn was no problem and it steadily mounted the post and then sent shoots off in all directions. I have since removed it but have kept the finger-thick spiral section which now adorns the front rockery, protruding from the neck of a wine bottle.

The third creeper is the smartest of the three. It goes up vertical surfaces on its own feet that attach to the surface in some way that makes them next to impossible to remove. Some of the 'feet' are meters long. There is one growing up the carport wall that has insinuated a foot through a gap a meter up the wall to the inside, then down the wall to a horizontal beam, along the beam another meter or so, then over the edge to under the beam, then down the vertical beam to the cement floor. Marvelous. I think that this plant is too smart to go to all this trouble just to get a foothold, as there are many other feet on the wall outside. My guess is that this foot, which looks like a piece of stout brown string, is also gathering nutrients and moisture.

Plants should get full marks for ingenuity, originality, extravagance, and variety – just like humans. There is a line of dense myrtles along my fence line thirty meters high. When the time had come to clear others that had self-sown under them, I was surprised to find a Camphor Laurel that had a trunk no thicker than my finger but three meters long! It was striving to find a place in the sun – just like we humans do. Plants are the basis for all animate life on the planet. We should take care of them all; not just the ones we use for food, medicines and clothing.

WE LIVING THINGS

One of the responses to the posting, *We Living Things,* was a query: at what stage does the soul enter the developing body, in the womb or later? I had an immediate unthought-through answer to the question about when the soul enterers the body but will not confess it immediately for it needs a preamble. (Of course, this question is of no interest if one chooses not to believe in a soul at all.)

According to various esoteric teachings the soul enters the body in different ways; it may be when the body is complete after the formation of the brain and nervous system, or at the first breath, or only partially until the seventh year after the faculties have been developed. There is a fourth possibility if one considers that all three are right, the soul gradually manifesting its presence until one is seven years old, with the faculties developed. This last one commends itself to reason. Ha! But therein lays the trap! From a higher perspective, all the answers are wrong. Why so? This is because they are an aspect of the dualistic thinking that characterizes the relative mind, thus automatically regarding body and soul as separate entities. Considering the ramifications of this it becomes apparent that this form of thinking is the cause of all our contradictions, arguments and confusion. The possible relationship between the dualities then becomes controversial and the pursuit of sciences and philosophy.

When opposites are regarded as absolute and duality rules, knowledge is divided into apparently conflicting principles. How does mind relate to matter? Matter to energy? Man to nature? God to man? And so on. In the light of higher wisdom, Western philosophy and science have struggled to bridge gaps that don't really exist; to unify parts of a single body and reconcile differences between opposites that are only apparent. This mental attitude was the main block to understanding the strange things that arose from the early experiments of atomic physics. The wiser Orientals, imbued with the realization that what appears to be in opposition, is in reality, complementary, had no such difficulty.

Consider the situation. Ignorant of most of life's deep mysteries, we are asking profound questions without noting that we insist that the answer must conform to our standards of reason and logic. This requirement severely limits the range of possibilities or totally obscures them. It means that any answer must conform to the ignorance that gave it birth.

With this preamble accepted it is now possible to consider an answer beyond common opinion, logic and reason, though not necessarily in conflict with them. Hence the ultimate answer is that the soul was ever-present and was the informing intelligence behind the whole process of gestation from conception to maturity. The process of growth from the zygote to death is a manifestation of the soul in matter. You see, we are much more wonderful than we can imagine. We do not know our own reality for equally profound reasons. This life is a game of hide-and-seek and in order for it to exist and continue to exist requires that the players be blindfolded; hoodwinked to the astounding truth. Lifetime after lifetime we catch a glimpse here, loose it there, get on with it, try to give it up, and finally get wise and start unraveling the binds and get bold enough to take the blindfolds off and know who we really are. Game over then, in ultimate freedom. "The Truth shall set you free".

Rather than being just an invention of mine the world's scriptures either hint at it or state it boldly, none more boldly than the Hindu Upanishads. The Self is equivalent to the Atman in that system or to our word, soul. This is a free rendering to which I have added a bit of local color:

Shvetaketu

At day's end, bright heat cooled, soothed away and muted
On sandalwood winds blown from Malay,
Between the sonorous seas
And the dappled ocean of sky, waved with cloud
From shore to shore,
Mynahs and crows caw, crying
Unseen in the Pepul trees,
And bulbuls singing in the palms;
Chatting white-striped squirrels gambol
Along the trunks, where the fire-flies scintillate
In the dark shadows...
To this chorus
The tinkling temple bells deck the air.
Blue wreathed incense rises.
To the cloistered chant of the Gayatri Hymn
The sun is sung down.
Birds settle in the Banyan branches.
At this slow cow-homing hour
The youth, Shvetaketu, sat bright faced,
Calm-hearted, poised as an angler,
Breath-baited,
Listening for the words of the teacher
Amongst this medley;
For some sound of that great song
Beyond the singing of life
In the evening...
...The sun set, bringing a sudden quiet.

When the lamps were lit in the ensuing silence,
The Guru spoke
To the listening presence of bright Shvetaketu.
"Shvetaketu, I hear by your silence
You have asked for our nation's wealth.
The knowledge to hear the unheard;
To perceive That beyond perception,
To know That beyond the known,
By which all things are known. Listen:
By knowing the substance clay,
All things made of clay are known,
The difference is only in word.
The truth of all such things is their clay-nature;
As by knowing that all gold things are nothing but gold,
No matter what their shape or purpose,
Such is that knowledge,
Knowing which, all else is known,
For It is one without a second.
It became all that is, Shvetaketu,
And all there is has its being in Him alone.
That is the subtle essence,
The Self of all,
And That, Shvetaketu,
That Thou Art!"
'Then", said Shvetaketu, "Tell me Sir, more about the Self."
"As the nectar gathered by the bees from many
Many flowers become one substance as honey
And one cannot define one separate flower in the honey,
Similarly all creatures, merged in one existence,
Whether in dreamless sleep or death,
Know nothing of a past or present state,
And do not know that they are merged in That.
Whatever creature, bright youth,
Elephant, tiger, gnat or worm,

Awake, dreaming or sleeping,
Have their being in That alone.
He is the subtle essence,
The Self of all,
And That Shvetaketu,
That Thou Art!"
"Then," said Shvetaketu, "Tell me, Sir, more about the Self"
"Strike at the root of the great Banyan tree.
Though it may bleed yet would it live.
Strike into its stem; lop off its top, yet it would live.
Supported by the living Self, the tree grows.
If the Self left a branch, that branch would die.
Likewise our body is like a log when the Self leaves it,
Though the Self does not die.
All that is, has its being in Him alone.
He is the subtle essence of all,
He is the Self,
And That, Shvetaketu,
That thou Art!"
'Please tell me more about this Self," begged Shvetaketu.
"So be it! Bring me the fruit from that Nyagrodha tree"
"Here it is Sir"
"Break it"
"It is broken"
"What do you see there?"
"Some very small seeds Sir"
"Break one of them"
"I have done so Sir"
"What do you see"
"Nothing Sir"
"The subtle essence you do not see,
And in that is the great Nyagrodha tree.
Like salt dissolved in water,
The Self cannot be seen within the body,

Though it abides there as the subtle essence.
Meditate, my son, on this-
When a person is dying, relatives gather round, saying,
"Do you know me?"
Until the speech is merged in mind,
And mind in breath, breath in prana,
The prana in the subtle essence,
Others can be known.
But when speech is merged in mind,
Mind in breath, breath in prana,
Prana in the Supreme Being,
Then they cannot be known.
In That which is the subtle essence
All beings have their existence.
That is the truth,
And That, Shvetaketu,
That Thou Art!"
Beyond the singing of life in the morning,
Shvetaketu and the Guru sat radiant-faced
In silence,
Listening to that one great song
Beyond the medley of early morning sound;
The tinkling temple bells like bright baubles,
Decked the morning air.

❧

It should be admitted that we live in a sensory world fraught with error and illusions and that our knowledge from a spiritual or ultimate point of view, can be regarded as a form of ignorance. The facts boggle the brain. For example, the actual location of everything in the universe is actually our own brain. This is the greatest mystery in all creation. It cannot ever be fathomed. The best that can be done is to say that an unknown something produces vibrations that are read in the language of each of the five senses as digitally programmed blips in nervous tissue. There are no pictures in the optic nerves, no sounds in the auditory nerves, no smells or tastes in the nerves of smell or taste, no skin, glass, hot or cold in the nerves of touch – only blips. We call the resulting electro-chemical events in the brain reality. It is the pattern of these blips in the brain that become the Universe. Actuality is beyond the scope of sensory data and the ignorance that is relative knowledge.

The only thing that can be called reality is the unknown something that all the ignorance is founded upon, for it is not relative, does not come and go, is not subject to change, has no birth or death, and is eternal, absolute and infinite. Its nature is eternal existence, absolute intelligence and infinite bliss. That is the real soul present throughout.

The logical, dualistic mind may ask; how come there are so many souls increasing every day in spite of wars, disease and disasters? Many other species are threatened with extinction, but the human animal is multiplying. Where do all these souls come from? Resorting again to esoteric doctrines the human being is an evolution from lesser life forms. I imagine the sequence to be something like the following - when an animal develops personality and a sense of identity it begins separating itself from the common mind of the herd, then incarnates as a primate and from that to an anthropoid and finally to a human. This is most often through incarnations as domestic animals and most of us have recollections of a pet that seemed next to human.

I knew one such and when we met there was an instant connection. I went to a farm to buy a horse and the dog, a Border-collie raced to meet me, tail wagging, jumping up, hand licking. The four-legged person followed me about and lay at my feet as we sat. The owners were most surprised as it was very unusual for their dog to behave like that. Shortly after, they phoned me saying that they were leaving and seeing that their dog took such a liking for me would I like to have her? When I went to pick her up I asked the dog's name. Didi, they said. When I opened the car door and called Didi she hopped in and as we drove home lay with her head on my lap. I wondered how it was that they called the dog Didi. Did they know that Didi is an affectionate appellation in the Bengali language added to the name of girls and women: Lakshmi-didi, Yogin-didi and so on? As to the possible reasons for this instant and unlikely connection I will leave it to the pleasure of your imagination. (PS. Who has seen the film, *Dean Spanley*? It's a classic for which Sam Neil should have got an Oscar.) Those of us who enjoy the frustrations of contemplating abstract notions might like to consider how this idea relates to Darwinian theories of evolution. Maybe it is reciprocal. The obverse truth; for if we have descended from anthropoids' then they must have ascended to us. But to continue the theme -

As the evolutionary process continues a sense of individuality is developed and the animal finally becomes a human with a strong sense of personal identity. At this stage spiritual evolution begins as the sense of a limited personal identity is slowly subsumed into a cosmic one. The ascent of anthropoids into a human status account for the great differences in human personality, from the basic first-born, through infinitive graduations of intelligence and abilities to the talented, gifted, geniuses, sages, saints and beyond. There may be no end to the evolutionary process, though there is as far as this planet is concerned, though according to some spiritual traditions, Hindu and Buddhist mainly, there are some illumined souls who, out of a spirit of compassion reincarnate in order to help individual souls towards freedom. If this explanation is unacceptable an alternative is that seeing each soul is a relative manifestation of an eternal and infinite consciousness, there can be no limit to how many, though I suspect that the same infinite consciousness would impose the needed restraints. We ourselves have managed to reduce the natural means of culling so with those removed up goes the birth rate - which is inevitable seeing that all things sexual are the major motivator of we living things. The Truth is beyond rational and logical belief.

SOUL AGAIN

My posts about the soul have created more than usual interest. The writer assumed the subject closed but discovered a writing that produced yet another post re the soul, but before beginning to explore this most recondite subject a cautionary tale should be told. There were two hyenas on a knoll scanning the plain below when one of them spotted a dead antelope. "Wow!" He said, "I can see a dead antelope; let's race down and eat it." "Hold on," said the older and wiser hyena, "We will stroll down and chew off as much as we can digest and leave the rest." There was a monkey on a tree above them who hearing this conversation, thought, "Yuk" - selecting a juicy berry off a nearby twig – "couldn't imagine anything worse."

What I discovered was written by Swami Vivekananda and taken from letters he wrote to the New York Morning Advertiser C 1895.

> *We may study all our lives and, in the end, fail to bring the problem of life and death to the plane of rational demonstration, affirmative or negative. We may talk or write, preach or teach for or against the permanence or impermanence of human existence as much as we like; we may become violent partisans of this side or that; we may invent names by the hundred, each more intricate than its predecessor and lull ourselves into a momentary rest under the delusion of our*

having solved the problem once and for all; we may cling with all our powers to any of the curious religious superstitions or the far more objectionable scientific superstitions – but in the end, we find ourselves playing an external game in the bowling alley of reason and raising intellectual pin after pin only for it to be knocked over again and again. Behind all this stands a fact unchallenged and unchallengeable – the inability of our mind to conceive our own annihilation. Even to imagine my own annihilation I shall have to stand by and look on as a witness.

This being so, the big question is: In the face of constant change, in nature without and the mind within, where does the notion of permanence come from? The ever-changing mind appears to inhabit an ever-changing body that is certainly not permanent. It must be very significant that we humans insist on regarding the ever-changing as permanent. In fact, the only thing that could be called permanent is constant change. To say the least, it is very weird.

In the letter quoted Vivekananda points out that there is another persistent idea we are subject to – our innate conviction that we are free; we can do as we determine, think as we want, are free to choose this or that. Are you convinced this is so? If you are bold enough to contemplate the subject, you may discover that like the notion of permanence it has no basis in fact. This is what another great Yogi, Sri Aurobindo has said:

The apparent freedom and self-assertion of our personal being to which we are so profoundly attached, conceal a most pitiable subjection to a thousand suggestions, impulsions and forces which we have made extraneous to our little person. Our ego, boasting of freedom, is at every moment the slave, toy and puppet of countless beings, powers, forces, influences and universal Nature.

According to the Vedanta philosophy espoused by the Swami these inexplicable notions are only resolvable by reference to a consciousness that does not change – it is our base state, Our Original Being – the Soul or Self. Though well explored both philosophically and described as experienced in the philosophy, the modern ideas about the soul are a curious mix. Its reality or nature is of little concern to most of us though as a familiar word there must be ideas attached to it; maybe in three different ways.

I suspect that the most common notion is that the soul is thought of as our ego or basic character, a congealed mass of personality, abilities, feelings, attitudes and proclivities. Though our basic self, it is composed of these bits, is impermanent and dissolves with the death of the body. Its adherents say 'when you die that's it. Kaput.

It's the easy option if the subject seems too abstract and difficult, so it is consigned to the too-hard basket. So the problem appears solved by denying it. It is the popular every-day attitude but is very limiting and personally I find it hard to believe anyone really believes it. If its adherents are convinced they are fundamentally nothing but a conglomeration of bits that is the end of the enquiry. One cannot expect to bother trying to understand a nonentity.

The next notion would most likely be the religious idea that the soul is a spark off an eternal flame and as such the living Core behind the conscious mind and so, life itself. To adherents of this belief the spark shares the immortality of its source and at the death of the body returns to its source in heaven. From this concept flow doctrines of God the Parent and humans as His (or Her) children and the curious idea that eternity begins at death. Most dualistic religions share some aspects of these ideas but say little or nothing about what the soul actually is.

There is another idea that could be shared by the scientifically minded and adherents of advanced schools of psychology and that is that the soul is the repository of all the accumulated experience of an individual that functions in the background of an individual's mind somewhat like software in a robot. It must follow WHY AND HOW MUST IT? that such a soul is an aspect of consciousness and in order to accumulate experiences must function in the background of various lives over time. The latter must be a necessary corollary in order to explain the differences in the powers of souls and why geniuses' and savants have knowledge and abilities from birth. (The psychiatrist Carl Jung had similar ideas to this which he developed from his interest in Indian teachings).

This concept makes a satisfactory introduction to the third possibility which is the one extolled by Vivekananda and taken from the non-dualistic teachings of Vedanta – a philosophy difficult to understand because of our inherent mode of dualistic thinking. Even an attempt at a description requires a compromise, so let's start with the previous concept of a sort of Core; a bedrock of the fruits of experience, understanding and knowledge often accepted as the nature of the soul. In Vedanta such a thing exists and is called the Jiva. This unsubstantial entity plays out as personality and character in the substantial world, becoming more unsubstantial and 'spiritual' as it evolves through many comings and goings. Just as a small patch of cloud can obscure the sun, so the relative mind obscures the knowledge of the soul; the Jiva then appears to be an ego in bondage to relative existence, subject to joy and suffering, old age and death.

This might be clear enough, but it is not clear at all, but the next idea is not easy to convey without some sort of dualistic error creeping in. How to say it? The Jiva is not the soul or the Core of Being *but must appear as such.* It is the reflection in mental matter of the real soul; the Absolute behind and within all that is relative, gross or subtle. Vedanta affirms that this or any other description is not real; merely an attempt to define the indefinable, explain the inexplicable, make credible the incredible. All attempts to rationalize the world-appearance through logical thought, by the individual ego, always ends in infinite regressions, contradictions and dead ends, as Advaita (non-dualistic) Vedanta affirms.

The confusion and arguments this way and that is because all these ideas hold just enough of the shadow of truth to be credible. In order to get an inkling of how things really are requires the ability to think in ultra-fine non-sensory abstractions, which might sound a strange request but thinking in abstractions that are of the intellect and not sensory, is what we do all the time. There would be no life without it, for nothing can be understood without reference to abstractions not obtained in the usual sensory ways. Such common ideas as matter, force, mind, time, space, and the concept of an absolute are all abstractions obtained by the mental process of generalization. They are called metaphysical because they are not primary data obtained through the senses; the usual foundation of physical knowledge.

These metaphysical concepts came relatively late in human development but were instinctively used by all creatures for millions of years before formulated. A raptor high aloft, effortlessly riding air currents, gliding exactly where it intends to be, knows nothing of the laws of aerodynamics but uses them with exquisite accuracy nonetheless. Neanderthals no doubt were aware of duration and the sequence of events and seasons without needing the concept of time – which in the 21st century rules our lives with the tyranny of a dictator. An aborigine fitting his woomera to his spear and launching it at a kangaroo with deadly accuracy knows nothing of trajectories, energy, mass, inertia, velocity or any of the abstractions that make it possible. Only a modern person without those skills can explain the scientific principles of how it is done by reference to metaphysical concepts. Both the ability to throw the spear with accuracy and the ability to describe the science of it are the imminent presence of an intelligence whose source is the soul. In contrast, some abstract concepts - such as freedom and permanence - cannot be demonstrated as realities in our sensory world. According to Vedanta they come from the real soul, called the Atman. These inherent human convictions veiled by the clouded mind are actually the dim presence of the soul filtered through nature.

As the presence of the sun in the cosmos makes life on earth possible, so the presence of the soul makes life in the world possible.

While the sages point out that descriptions of the non-dual must all be faulty the nature of the Atman as pure, permanent, free, absolute, infinite and eternal are derived from the presence of their opposites in the relative world because change presupposes changeless, the impure purity, bondage, freedom, the finite the infinite, the temporal eternity. None of these absolutes are a feature of ordinary consciousness. The hindrance to understanding the Atman as it relates to relative life is that such descriptions presume it to be a compound; a mix of these amorphous things, though it is a Unity beyond relative ideas. To those who know the world the Absolute is non-existent; to those who know the Absolute, the world is non-existent. Such is the mystery. Reality is difficult to comprehend but can be realized in higher states of consciousness. The great yogi Shankara (AD 788-820) describes this highest state of consciousness:

The ego has disappeared. I have realized my identity with Brahman, and so all my desires have melted away. I have risen above my ignorance and my knowledge of this seeming universe. What is this joy that I feel? Who shall measure it? I know nothing but joy, limitless, unbounded!

The ocean of Brahman is full of nectar – the joy of the Atman. The treasure I have found there cannot be described in words. The mind cannot conceive of it. The mind fell like a hailstone into that vast expanse of Brahman's Ocean. Touching one drop of it, I melted away and became one with Brahman. And now, as I return to human consciousness, I abide in the joy of the Atman. Where was this universe? Who took it away? Has it merged in something else? A while ago I beheld it – now it exists no longer. This is wonderful indeed! Here is the ocean of Brahman, full of endless joy. How can I accept or reject anything? Is there anything distinct or apart from Brahman? Now, finally and clearly I know that I am the Atman whose nature is eternal joy. I see nothing, I hear nothing, I know nothing that is separate from me.

That amazing transcendental experience is the realization of the soul, the end point of human evolution. The dedicated souls who have realized themselves affirm that the Atman is the only permanent and free, unshackled, changeless.

The Supreme Soul abides in the realm of the heart, though it manifests the universe. From It are born the five elements, the enjoyer and the enjoyed, energy, mind and body. Hence It supports all beings. It is immortal and glorious. All beings are born in It and at death merge into It once more. So great is It that It supports the earth, heaven, the universe, soul, and God. (From the Mahabharata)

In the Sanskrit language its nature is *sat chit ananda* - Absolute Existence, Intelligence and Bliss and the marvelous thing is that though it cannot be known by the dualistic mind, it can be realized. It is the Divine; not in some antiseptic heaven but our own intrinsic nature; the Self of us all, beyond the birth and death of the Jiva.

Understanding these mysteries of life though, is not only an intellectual undertaking. It requires dedication, persistence and the courage to take an existential leap off the springboard of the known – in the religious context, a leap of faith.

Well, that's it. The Last Word.

CATSH 22

Without prior intention I created a sort of fable that I can trace to a thought at least fifty years old. It began when I was cleaning some cat shit off my bathroom floor and gagging at the terrible stench. "Nice of them to bury it" I thought. Amongst a trillion forgotten things lost in the far depths of consciousness this experience popped out while I was writing a letter to a friend and launched me off into a piece of nonsense that probably made her think I had gone bonkers. Anyhow, out it came and down it went and was sent as part of an otherwise normal letter. Later, I tinkered with it a bit and added a title pinched from Heller's famous novel, 'Catch 22'. The reason I like it so much is because it is so silly. I wish I could write at least one a week, but alas, the Muse is not so kind.

Long ago, when cats were first invented, all the other animals were in a state of shock and resentment because of the fact that cat poop smelt so awful. As the dogs were the most incensed at this outrage, having such a keen sense of smell, they sent a representative Up to complain to the Lord High Creator, (LHC).

'Look here, Lord!' barked the dog; 'of all your creatures we dogs have the best sense of smell which makes those cats impossible to live with!'

It was wise of the animals to send a dog, as they are the most articulate and political of animals.

'One poop and the whole forest stinks for days!' he continued. 'Our whole social system is in a turmoil – we can't sniff out our trails, mark our territories, know who is who, or smell a rabbit from on top of the warren. Even the eagles are complaining! Fleas were bad enough, but we canines reckon You have gone too far this time!'

'Oh goodness me,' exclaimed the LHC, 'tsk tsk, what could I have been thinking about? – Something very cosmic, I suppose.... Just a moment and I will look up the Akashic record...'

She fiddled with the cosmic knobs. The whole sky lit up with the words, CAT (tortoiseshell, tabby etc.) with sketches and plans for the various models. Then the words NATURE, PLACE IN THE ECOLOGY, ETC, with all the appropriate listings.

'Well, all seems to be in order' She said.

Meanwhile Dog was getting very impatient. He started pacing up and down, growling under his breath.

'But let Us see the finer detail,' continued the LHC, tapping away on the heavenly console. The sky of heaven – which reaches all the way from the Beginning to the End – was lit up with the words FELINE BIOCHEMISTRY. All the biochemical cascades peculiar to cats flashed upon the heavens.

'Look here, Dog, said the LHC, 'everything seems to be in order. Are you sure it is not the humans who are causing the problem?'

At this Dog reached the limits of his restraint. 'Humans?' he barked, 'why, we dogs are the only friends they have! No! It's those sneaking, vermin loving, snobbish cats You created who are upsetting all creaturedom. The monkeys are so busy holding their noses that they fall out of the trees. The birds can't fly because they need a wing to cover their beaks. This is serious!'

Exasperated, Dog lost control and jumped and yelped and growled and barked.

'Down with all cats we dogs say!' He stood with head down, tongue out, panting, utterly exhausted with Righteous Indignation.

'Dear dear, now then...' said the LHC, 'you dogs are apt to get excited over nothing.'

'Nothing!' The dog cried, shedding angry tears.

'Sit down and behave yourself 'She said, 'SIT I say!'

Though the dog had not attended obedience school, he sat, glowering at the heavens, exasperated. Frustrated beyond endurance he presumed to instruct Her.

'Try the alimentary tract!' he barked.

'Very well then,' She said, 'If that will keep you quiet.'

Up came the words ALIMENTARY TRACT, cats for the use of.

There followed line after line of chemical symbols denoting enzymes, organisms and the like.

But then, three lines appeared blank!

The LHC blushed and said, 'Ahem!' and looked so sheepish Dog stood up and barked.

'Oh dear,' said the LHC, 'it appears I have slipped up somewhere. Just look at that! Two organisms missing from the bowel and one enzyme from the pancreas. NO WONDER THEIR SHIT STINKS TOO MUCH! What could I have been thinking of?'

She tapped the question into the computer. The heavens were lit with the words BUSY WITH EARLY WINTER IN EUROPE AND THE TOO SOON MIGRATION OF THE CRESTED PLOVER FROM SIBERIA TO AUSTRALIA.

'Of course, of course,' said the LHC, 'not a moment to spare! I was so busy it taxed My omnipotence, I remember,' and She disappeared. The dog stood up, sniffed and looked about, ears cocked.

The LHC appeared before the Dog in Her nicest human form, wearing an old dressing gown, fluffy slippers and carrying a big bone. In Her sweetest tones She said, 'dear Dog, you are completely correct and it was I who was at fault. After all, nobody is perfect. However, not to worry, I shall think of some sort of solution. Go back and tell everybody I will fix it somehow. And not only that, I will give dogdom a boon as well,' She said, tickling his ears.

Somewhat placated by all this, dog wagged his tail, took the bone and bounded off.

After some thought the LHC called the Cat Spirit up and confessed all that had happened, with all sorts of explanations and apologies as well.

She said,' What's done is done. There is no use crying over spilt milk. Catdom must help Me out of this most embarrassing situation by promising not to tell anyone. But from this time on, all cats must bury it as soon as it is done. You have strong claws, so it will be no trouble to dig a little hole - but it must be done right away mind you. Now, if you do that, I will give you a very special boon. What do you say?'

"Prrrrrr' said the Cat Spirit, brushing itself up against Her legs with a friendly little nuzzle, 'I think we can arrange that, prrrrr. But what about the boon?' Cat rubbed its cheeks against Her slippers.

'How about plenty of mice for All-time and a major role in Zoology?' said the LHC.

'Thank you,' the Cat Spirit said, 'but what about us keeping the secret? If we let it slip to just one flea, the whole world will know in no time flat.' The Cat Spirit purred and rolled over in the most beguiling way, nuzzling the feet of the LHC and rubbing itself along Her ankles in such an ingratiating manner that the LHC had a warm fuzzy all over.

'Hmm. Yes, I see your point, 'She said. 'I do like cats...How about I make humans dote on you cats, how's that?'

'That will do very nicely.' said the cat, stalking off, tail in the air, without so much as a goodbye or backward glance.

Which is why cats are so smug, dogs are so joyous, cats bury it as soon as it is done, dogs hate cats, and there are so many mice.

SUBVERTING PARADIGMS

(The whole truth about sex)

Graffiti is a sign of the times. When I was a lad eighty years ago, the messages were down to earth or naive. They read 'Down with scabs' or merely 'FOO was here!' Single words were popular. The word 'Eternity' adorned city pavements in fine scroll and many walls bore the mysterious personal pronoun 'FOO' and nothing else.

When I read graffiti announcing that 'Sex is better than logic, but I can't prove it', I knew the turning point had come. The trend culminated in a recent sighting, on a lavatory wall usually reserved for lewd and vulgar affirmations, the advice to *'Subvert the dominant paradigm'*. After going home to consult a dictionary for the meaning of the words, I realized that subverting was a tendency of mine; so these words are dedicated to the author of this anarchistic demand. It is high time the pervasive paradigm, Sexuality is Essential, was brought under suspicion. At the outset, it would be foolish to deny the truths of our long history. Unlike other species, the wheels of our reproductive cycles are in perpetual motion. As sexual athletes some members of our species make rampant stags look lethargic.

The French author, Georges Simenon, the creator of Inspector Maigret, was out of sorts if he didn't make it a few times a day, preferably with more than one partner. Paris in the roaring twenties provided plenty of opportunity. One of his consorts was the energetic Josephine Baker, who was capable of outstripping even him, by his own confession. Since then, sexual preoccupations have escalated to pervade our culture as salt does the sea. It is implicit, explicit, subliminal, overt, covert, or perverted. The flood of it all may be ultimately non-productive as the inevitable ennui sets in. Hallelujah! It'll be time for a change!

But actions and reactions simply cause the pendulum to swing now this way, now that. The heavy sexual restraints that were the vogue in the 1820's were under pressure in the 1920's, capitulating in the sixties. The sexual revolution became the modern thing, thus securing its status; the words modern and good having become synonymous.

The power of sex became the major means of manipulating people as the advertising industry came to dominate the media. That finally put sexuality in the daily diet of everyone, along with foods eaten because they go Snap Crackle and Pop. Once the word *bed* was associated only with the words *sleep, rest* or perhaps *sick* - nowadays the word *sex* would have to be included and the word *sexy* is now a laudatory adjective, indiscriminately applied - even to motor cars. *Fuck,* now replaces *bloody* as the most commonly used expletive, often gratuitously jammed into sentences as *bloody* never was - no one ever said with an aggressive tone, 'Where *the bloody* are you going'?

The term '*making* love' has now given way to '*having* sex'. Attitudes are now so perverted that even affection shown a child can be suspect. Trivial signs perhaps, but like a stiff neck, a cough and a sniffle they may indicate the presence of a malady.

Hopefully, excesses may finally lead to boredom or shock as the toll begins to be clearly visible. No doubt, we will again call the swing of the pendulum in the opposite direction a revolution. Perhaps we will see a little clearer and be prepared to admit that the promotion of sexuality and promiscuous sex has become the major social and personal problem. When the conspiracy of silence about its insidious effects comes to an end, an honest appraisal will reveal the fact that random sex may be more like a bed of nails than a bed of roses.

There may be too much of it or not enough, addictively fulfilling or a mere sneeze in the loins, a boring chore, a terrible compulsion, an addiction, or at best, a mutually joyful fulfilment bonding couples for decades. Sex can invite unhealthy excesses tempting us into too many misadventures fraught with all sorts of dangers. From the back seat it may drive our most crucial decisions, the results often causing deep regrets, revealing that it is not love that is blind, but lust. The much vaunted sexual freedom can become just another form of bondage.

Sex is as unreliable as our fantasies about it. Those we lust for one day may boor us soon after. It may promise dreams it cannot fulfil, and is tainted with every illusion demented desires are prone to. In our lives and minds sex can be a thrashing morass of confusions, whirling love and lust, fear and fulfilment, repulsion and longing, freedom and bondage, terrible compulsions and serene feelings, energy or ennui, appearing now one, now the other, like clothes in the window of a tumble dryer.

So much for the dominant paradigm. And all this is without mention of syphilis, gonorrhoea, AIDS, chlamydia, thrush, herpes, or the dangers of oral contraceptives. More bad news for sex addicts is that science may soon be capable of making coitus obsolete – harvest an ovum and a squirt of semen; culture them in an artificial womb and wait nine months. If not impressed with their own gene pool surrogate parents will be able to select donors from what males and females in the program they admire most, selecting for qualities and abilities they expect their non-biological children to inherit. Either way, the whole messy business of coitus, gestation, morning sickness and childbirth may one day be done away with; just another advantage in the Brave New World.

While a rampant generation is fornicating with no discretion, commitment or love, this obsession with sexual freedom is profitable for manufactures of contraceptives, new-age teachers, the porn industry, sex workers and webcam voyeurs, doctors, psychologists and psychiatrists. It's an ill wind that doesn't blow to someone's advantage but it is the same wind that helps keep the kite flying.

Psychiatrist's paradigms about sex, powered by Freud's neurosis more than truth, have, to say the least, perverted the course of justice. Though I have a penis of sorts, I am not prepared to believe that this piece of tubing dangling from my loins is likely to cause envy in anyone. At this point I wish to record that in my estimation this piece of very sensitive tubing and its pouch of tender testicles is nature's standing joke on the male gender, being hung out in a most vulnerable place where it is likely to be pierced by prickly bushes, hanging within easy reach of even small dogs. For elegance, simplicity and discretion the female model is hard to beat. To add insult to injury males also have hair growing out of their face as well.

Having now mentioned gender, I think that the outcome of rampant sexual activity has different effects for men and women. Women can be augmented by it, men depleted. At each ejaculation a man loses some of his vital energy and lots of nutrient rich sperm, which the woman absorbs into her blood stream along with some of his vital energy. It must be significant that girls have a full set of ovum at birth yet boys have no sperm until the testicles descend at puberty and that it is the male that determines gender with either a Y or X chromosome. Why have women so many erogenous zones and a huge clitoris that extends from the outer bud down to each side of the vagina? Why is the sperm count of ejaculate greatly decreasing? Why is homosexuality increasing exponentially? Why is there hair on the pubes? Why is it that of all mammals, only females of some apes and all humans menstruate? There are many mysteries still open to speculation, but escalating gender confusion is a fact. The avalanche of ingested plastics is confusing our biochemistry with hormone-imitating molecules from plastics in can linings and drink bottles, so a high percentage of girls are now having their menses before their teens and some boys are developing breasts. Maybe we are headed for an androgynous society, or maybe an effeminate one; as if we don't have enough problems to contend with already.

To my mind Freud's biggest error was the notion that religion was a substitute for sex. This should be turned the right way around. Our obsession with sex becomes a substitute for true religion. Unlike its comparison with logic, I think this can be proved. Apparently Freud could not think of religion as being anything but belief in dogma, a particular Messiah, a certain ritual. These too, can be a substitute for real religion. The word comes from roots meaning to bring together. This does not mean to come together as in a congregation only, but to bring all one's energies together, to gather oneself up, to be entire, integrated, concentrated. This requires dedication and a stripping away of every complication. Whenever the sex urge rules one's life, real religion is not possible.

Yet our most powerful urge is towards complete physical, psychic and spiritual union; the urge that sanctifies marriage. No amount of fornication or copulation can ever compensate for the lack of this spiritual dimension. The joy of this consummation is the closest the ordinary person can come to the transcendental joy of divine communion.

The old Hindus knew this and celebrated a spiritual sexuality in the schools of Tantra Yoga. It is a strict and difficult discipline that has nothing to do with sexual satisfactions. However, what is called Tantric sex in the West may give a master of the art the ability to extend coitus indefinably, giving a partner supreme delight and ejaculating or not at will. Women can learn to constrict the vagina in pulses to give the same sensations of pleasure to the male, but this sounds like making something already fulfilling just too good not to be addicted too.

Tantra acknowledges that the sex urge in its many manifestations was the driving force of creation in all its forms and that this energy came from the sun. In Konarak on the east coast is the famous 13th Century Sun Temple, a huge edifice carved from sand stone in the form of a chariot with twelve huge wheels and life size horses and two attendant elephants. It abounds in marvellous carvings of twining plants, erotic figures copulating in all positions, with celestial musicians and dancers celebrating life and procreation. The temple symbolizes the chariot of life moving through time and space energised by sexual energy and the sun. Nothing lascivious here, though typically, the first English visitors were shocked (perhaps fascinated too) but having dirty minds, decided to be disgusted. Similarly there is nothing lascivious in the famous Kama Sutras. It is a rather clinical manual of various aspects of sexuality, but well worth a read.

According to the metaphysics of Yoga, celibacy causes radical modifications of the nervous system, making possible transcendental realizations and finally, knowledge of the ultimate reality. Sperm contains a powerful spiritual essence *(Ojas)* and like money, can't be stored up if constantly spent. The storing up of Ojas is the real purpose behind the practise of celibacy. Hence every religion has advocated a chaste life or celibacy for those who are in earnest. If Georges Simenon's rampant sexual energy had been transmuted he would be transformed into an enlightened sage well before the usual time it takes of twelve years. Repression is just as destructive as obsession. They are troubles both. Sublimation isn't. It is the creative alternative. Plenty of celibates have known it. All seventeen of Sri Ramakrishna's inner circle of disciples were celibates who led free and dedicated lives and some of his householder disciples did as well. In this funny old world where things are often topsy-turvy, it is only the dedicated celibate who may realize the ultimate bliss. This is exemplified in the suffix *ananda* (bliss) to the monastic names of those in the Swami order. It is sad that Catholic priests are not disciplined in the Yoga methods of transmuting this powerful urge.

Swami Turiyananda was amazed when his Guru, the Avatar Sri Ramakrishna, told him to increase his lust. When he expressed his surprise the Master said, 'What is lust? It is the desire to get. Then desire to get the greater fulfilment in God and strengthen this desire greatly.' Turiyananda, once said, 'There must be a psychology of lust, and what is that? It is the desire to attain oneness. Lust is also an aspect of that love. But men take the wrong course. They get stuck at the gross, and fail to carry it up to the pure substance, God.' But Ramakrishna often affirmed that lust and greed were the locks on the chains that bind us.

Most of us prefer the excitement of sex and its momentary satisfactions to the challenge of celibacy and the discovery of the unknown. Yet, if union with one's lover can be so engrossing, think what union with the ultimate Being must be like. Though celibacy might be the creative alternative, to do it, the whole life style has to be a paradigm buster, so it should appeal to iconoclasts and individualists. Gandhi was one such. Though married, he became celibate at 37 in order to devote all his creative energy to the task he had set himself.

George Bernard Shaw said that marriage was popular because it combined the maximum temptation with the maximum opportunity, yet when all the puffing and blowing of exploiting the temptation has faded, as it surely must, marriage provides an excellent opportunity to practice celibacy. Another idea that needs to be undermined is the popular notion that if our sexual life is denied we go a bit bonkers, but the truth is, many people live happy lives free of the need for sex, but they don't get any publicity. Maybe the truth is that promiscuous and licentious people are a bit bonkers already.

Celibacy should be promoted as a healthy alternative and part of a cultured and disciplined life, as it once was. People need to be able to practice celibacy without feeling that they are going against the laws of health or alienating themselves from society. This includes the few young who are wise enough to want to avoid the demeaning effects of promiscuity or its dangers; the matured who have no desire for random sex without love, or the dedicated scientist, researcher or spiritual aspirant who have no time for sexual pursuits and the complications it invites into their lives, because every original creative realization in art, engineering, architecture, literature, philosophy, religion or science is fed by some of this fundamental energy.

Even sexual deprivation need not be the cause of terrible frustrations, but an opportunity to practice an art as old as sex itself – creative celibacy! Any takers? No?...Then don't be a Glug, try to find some other paradigm to subvert instead.

The Glug Quest

Meditate deeply on soft goods or sex,
On caraway seeds or the causes of bills,
Biology, art or mysterious wrecks,
Or the tattered white fleeces of clouds on blue hills.
Muse upon ologies, freckles and fog,
Why hermits live lonely and grapes in a bunch,
The ways of a child or the mind of a dog,
Or the oyster you bolted last Friday at lunch.
Throw wide the portals and let your thoughts run
Over the earth like a galloping herd
Bounds to profundity let there be none,
Let there be nothing too madly absurd.
Ponder on pebbles or stock exchange shares,
On the mission of man or the life of a bug,
On planets or billiards, policemen or bears,
Alert all the time for a sight of a Glug.

C.J. Dennis, *The Glugs of Gosh.*

HOLES ARE WHOLES

I ask you: where would we be without holes? Doubtless the wonderful and mysterious nature of holes has not dawned upon you. They are overlooked as the most important things in life. In fact there could be no life without them, considering that if there were not two holes in your nose you could not breath and if there were not another immediately below them there would be no way to introduce life giving food into the other chain of holes in tubes that make up the body.

Cups and glasses and all sorts of containers are holes in various sorts of matter: right? If those holes with bases didn't exist there would be nothing to put things in; think of how terribly inconvenient that would be. Holes in all their marvellous variety are more essential to life than matter is because it is only the holes in matter that make life possible.

Here's another thing – holes are absolute. They come in wholes because you can't have half a hole. Everyone is complete no matter what shape it is or how big. The numerical nought is really an empty hole with a ring around it but where would mathematics be without it?

And what's more, all life depends upon tubes and tubes are nothing more than elongated holes and so are pipes for things to go down and tunnels for trains to go through. So you see, nothing is just as important as something. Holes are nature's most incredible invention. And that's not the whole story either. All life involves tubes. It is one of nature's basic inventions around which all the others depend. The long convoluted one that starts at the mouth might be as huge as an elephant's or whale's or as minute as a flea's. Its sole purpose involves food - which is another word for world because everything here is or becomes food for something else.

It is another strangeness that no matter what food for any creature might be, it is useless as is. Once in the tube it has to be broken down, separated into its constituent bits and then reassembled into chemicals whose interactions produce the energy through which the critter, mouse or man, can go and win more things to stuff into the tube in order to get enough energy to do it all over again. This is strange enough, but putting cooked, assembled things into the tube might be done in company with ceremony, even pomp, but the inevitable outcome is done alone behind closed doors.

Here is another mysterious fact: all this incredible variety of whatever is food for whatever animal, is ultimately nothing more than solar energy trapped into plants by photosynthesis. We human animals are proud of our ability to discover so much about it all, but usually accept the facts without question. But I ask: 'How come? Why?' How come we have to go through all these biochemical complications so intricate that bodies keep going awry or become diseased – instead of obtaining our energy directly and simply like a photocell can?

The only answer I can think of is that nature has invented something analogous to a clock, powered by the spring of solar energy, the actions of little cogs and wheels hidden behind the face, turning the big hands of hours and minutes to tell stories in time. As far as I can see, all of nature is a devious plot to keep every life form on the planet locked into the process of keeping the little cogs and wheels acting, so big wheels we can only dimly surmise keep turning. It is all so weird that if it didn't exist it would be impossible to imagine it.

An attempt to visualize what life would be like if all creatures did not have to eat food is a challenge to one's imagination. Perhaps you might be tempted to try to imagine a life free from the need to eat. Obviously, there would be no agriculture, animal husbandry and abattoirs, nor conflicts for arable land. Imagination would tempt us to dream altruistic utopias. I can see a possibility of how this might come about, for all life has but five processes – digestion, assimilation, distribution, elimination and procreation – all except the last directly concerned with the processing of food.

This is how it might be - ancient Oriental cultures taught that the organ systems were also active on a metaphysical level. In this way the energy giving the small intestine its abilities also made possible the mental ability to assimilate experience; the bowel to eliminate unnecessary data, emotions and digested facts, and so on. So it can be inferred that if these five abilities were freed from the restraint of processing material substances, that they would then become available for higher, more subtle processes, ultimately freeing us from our mental, emotional and spiritual inadequacies as experience could be properly digested, assimilated and understood and the limiting and false speedily eliminated. Procreation would then become the ability to create children that express our innate potentials in greater measure. That's the closest I can come to an idea of a practical utopia.

A transformation of our vital processes from processing food to the clarification of consciousness could be the endpoint of physical evolution. Perhaps such an elevation of our vital processes is behind the religious discipline of fasting. I have tried fasting many times for up to three days on nothing but water and once on only a little brown rice which I found much harder. I found that nothing was easier than nothing but rice. What is hunger but the sensation of having an empty tube? Apart from hunger, all I experienced was a pleasant lightness of being and a clearing of the Big Tube. And a saying – there is nothing slower than a fast.

There is plenty of data to show the benefits of fasting for short periods, some researchers declaring that a 24 hour fast once a week could add 10 years to the life span which is another good reason the treat fasting with caution. On this subject it is worth pointing out that busy people who lunch at midday, skip an afternoon snack and have their evening meal at seven have fasted for seven hours and those who neglect breakfast and a morning tea snack, similarly. This is not a bad idea once a week or twice a week depending on the workload. The number of grossly obese people waddling about is an indication of how unpopular any form of fasting is and how popular gorging on junk food has become. The extra strain on all the tubes inevitably leads to disease and early death.

Vegans are the opposite and there is no such thing as a fat one. So what it all boils down to is the startling revelation that seeing there is no such thing as half a hole they must all be wholes and because tubes are only long holes they must be wholes as well; no doubt about it, life is really holey.

THE ART OF CREATIVE IMAGING

Considering the many vicissitudes, we encounter throughout life; we humans are heroes. In our life there is disease, various sufferings, disaster, problems, frustrations and other difficulties and then inevitably, old age, sickness and death. Yet we soldier on regardless. Thousands bravely endure ghastly or even terrible lives, many others sad and difficult ones. Admitting these facts is not being negative; just telling like it is. If you deny this aspect of life, you're an optimist, if you think it outweighs the good bits, you're a pessimist. I remember an exchange between my parents that went something like this – *Blimey Anne, your nothing but a pessimist! What do you expect, living with an optimist all my life?* I suppose most of us are a bit of both.

In one way or another, life can be difficult for us all no matter how secure and well-off we might be. We then fear that such comfort might be lost. We all know that at the start of each day adversity in one form or another might hit us though we find it best not to give it any thought. The old adage 'count your blessings and smile' is sage wisdom but sometimes not so easy to do. Nevertheless, blessings are always there, even if you have to imagine them for a future time.

This opens up new ideas to explore – the creative use of this fascinating aspect of mental activity – imagination. It is commonly thought to be the ability to conceive subtle, original or outlandish images strung together to make a theme or story. So it can be said of a person so dull as to lack the ability, 'they have no imagination' though no one can be alive and not live by imagination because every thought, word or feeling and therefore all experience, is a mental image. In this sense everything we know is resolvable to an image as *image*-ination. This being so, it is a sobering thing to consider that everything we know about ourselves and the world, sun and moon and whatever, only exist as images in consciousness.

If this is so, it must range from the inputs from all the senses to attitudes, emotions and opinions as well. Though the senses are commonly ascribed to the presence of an external reality, in the final analysis, they must become internal images. The internal world they create and our individual attitude to it are the basis for everything else in the psyche. The sensory world we experience becomes overlaid - sometimes even created by - our notions and attitudes. Together they create our personal world. In that case our personality appears to be merely a figment of our own imagination, but the external world a reality. You might ask, so what? But thinking on it, you will see that though radically changing the nature of the supposed external world is not possible, changing your attitude to it is within your grasp. It is not too difficult to see that what we call thinking is imaging. Even abstract thinking is attended by nebulous images through which meaning is expressed. In this sense everything is imagination. The images we believe in not only govern our lives; they *are* our lives. In the final analysis our life is made from ideas. A famous sage has written:

> All individuals *by their very nature* are free from living, old age and death, though they *imagine* that they are subject to them by the power of thought. They then deviate from their true nature. That which appears to exist on the strength of false knowledge *based upon imagination* does not really exist. Our true nature transcends all limitations. It is ever free and action less, indivisible and absolute. In

it there is no concept of cause and effect. It is absolute reality, *beyond imagination.*

Sounds a bit radical doesn't it? Imagine knowing this for sure! Believe it or not, some heroes have, and some do, but they are not ordinary heroes like you and me. Not content to stop there they say that when all imaging ceases then there is a constant state of causeless joy and that this free state is the culmination of our heroic evolution. Well, that's some consolation I suppose for we who are still in the difficult process of getting there – or trying to avoid it.

There is another old saying that as art follows life, so life follows art, and many believe so. I wonder then, if life and art have a reciprocal relationship, what is the effect of the plethora of ugly imaginings we are confronted with in the arts – particularly films. If the saying is true, 'taking in' these images isn't making life any less grim, ugly or traumatic, but amplifies the possibility of them all, by fixing them into the mind of the world. On the other hand, it is certainly beneficial therapy to creatively imagine the good for yourself, others and the planet, affirming the positive, beneficial aspects from life's range of possibilities.

The old saying might seem a bit trite these days, but we *are* what we think. This might seem to be an inescapable bind, yet imagination can also be the mental tool that can produce beneficial mental effects that free us from mental bondage. As prayer or meditation, it is as old as the hills. We are all hypnotised by the known (images) and meditation is the process of de-hypnotising ourselves. Being bold, using the faculty of imagination creatively might be the way out from what Shakespeare called 'the slings and arrows of outrageous fortune'. The only use for the troubles that plague us is to drive us towards this effort to transcend them as the only and final solution to the challenge and difficulties of being alive.

Such efforts are wilfully opposed by most individuals, because it is seen as a threat to their individuality as an ego - as indeed it is. It takes great maturity to be aware of the fact that we worship our own images more than anything else. To this extent we are all image worshippers, no matter how abstract our notions of a God may be, for even the most abstract, nebulous idea is an image. The exclusive, obstinate worship of such images, internal or external, gives rise to fanaticism. The fanatic must force their opinion upon others because they are darkly aware that the truth is other than they imagine. Fanaticism is overcompensating for suspected ignorance and secret doubts. Curiously, fanaticism is due to a limitation of the faculty of imagination. It is imagination stuck in a rut. It is wisdom not to believe everything one thinks. Materialistic, worldly people on the other hand, are also victims of inhibited imagination. The more a person holds dogmatically to their self-made materialistic ideas and images, the less they are capable of imagining altruistic, mystical or spiritual ones. They then tend to deny anything abstract, religious or altruistic, and so suffer a self-imposed blight of the faculty of imagining. If the idea that everything in life is mere imagination is presented to the ordinary person, and they were asked to comment upon it, what would be the likely response? Whatever it might be, they would have to review their stock of images to provide an answer. They would react according to their opinions, attitudes, conditioning, conclusions, knowledge and ignorance - all images in consciousness. There would be very few that would not condemn it as ridiculous. If they were then asked what was the nature of all this imaging and in what substance it was taking place, the most common response would be that it was the mind. If it was pointed out that such an answer was pure imagination, for the mind as an entity in its own right is never an object of experience, but an inference based upon the memory of having thoughts and feelings confirmed by a common consensus, no doubt they would tend to become belligerent. But maybe it is so. As another old saying goes, truth is stranger than fiction.

Imagination is a marvellous faculty. Creative imagination can be fun, with no other purpose than to exercise the faculty and while away the time. If you have to experience lock-down or isolation again, trying to imagine how the first discoveries came about could take days. Way back in our pre-Neanderthal past, or in it, someone must have discovered how to make fire at will instead of waiting for a lightning strike. Did some extra smart one look at two pieces of wood and think "I reckon if I rub those two together they would get so hot a bit of dry moss would catch fire to keep us all warm." And that could start a chain reaction leading to investigating all the ways we have learnt to strike a light; from the friction method to the flint and steel to matches and gas to electricity. But that's no fun because it is a matter of recorded history. After making fire became commonplace the next thing must have been cooking. Who was the first cook? There was no pan or pot because that needed the first person to make a pot from clay. How did firing it come about? Who was the first person to ride a horse or an elephant and how come? What artisan made the first shoe; invented metallurgy; burnt coke; made a bow and arrow; wove material; died it? The list gets to be endless. Imagine those millions of people who watched the heavy lid of a pot move up under the pressure of steam for centuries before one of them imagined making a steam engine. We owe a debt of thanks to them all. I reckon there should be a yearly celebration called the First Persons Festival in memory of all these unknown human benefactors who creatively used the faculty of imagination.

THE BIG (NON) BANG AND THE BEGINNING OF US.

The following thoughts are due to an accident. I bought a hard cover book at a stall it the markets because it had an interesting title. t cost only a dollar, so I had nothing to lose. It purports to explain the process by which the universe came to be. It is titled 'The First Three Minutes'.

The revolution Einstein, Bohr, Schrodinger and Plank started, produced quantum mechanics, the atom bomb and incredible speculations about the beginning of the universe, now called the 'standard model' – Big Bang to you and me. It seems to me that the tendency for speculations to become creeds or even dogma is the danger of science, as it has in religion and philosophy. It seems that this has happened to the Big Bang *theory*. Providentially, someone might unearth other data and the theory might be consigned to the overflowing dustbin of discarded scientific theories; so as clever as it is, it is not set in cement. Adherents are adamant that what they speculate to have taken place is as the theory predicts. Such cosmological divinations are amazing and a credit to the persevering intellect, imagination, and creativity of the scientific mind.

These days, the first morning hours during which I consume my two mugs of tea, are spent reading about what happened after the Big Bang. Briefly, the first three minutes of the universe goes something like this: ***BANG.*** That is, a mighty explosion of we don't know what. This bang had no specific starting point such as all lesser worldly explosions, but happened spontaneously everywhere at the same time, though just before the Bang there was no time and no everywhere either. (I suppose this means that the Bang occurred in eternity and the everywhere in infinity). It is necessary to ignore the fact that there could not have been any time at the time, nor a somewhere or an everywhere - and that it could not have gone Bang as this hypothetical event happened billions of years before Ears.

It was incredibly hot – one hundred thousand million degrees centigrade to be exact, pouring out unbelievably vast numbers of the four basic particles: electrons, positrons, neutrinos and photons. (Photons? In simple terms this could be expressed as: “Let there be light.”)

The authorities declare that this event ‘filled all space with every particle rushing apart from every other particle’ - though where the space came from is not mentioned. (Maybe they mean infinity).To avoid the problem of the on-existent everywhere getting jammed up with these particles, as many as created were instantly annihilated (so here appears one of the universe’s basic processes – dynamic stability.) All this happened in the first 100th part of a second though of course there were no seconds (being our invention) though I suppose some sort of duration must have begone to allow for a sequence of events.

All explosions start out super-hot and then cool down - even the original one - so after all this activity of coming and going of bits had been going on for one tenth of a second the temperature had dropped down to a mere thirty thousand million degrees centigrade. After fourteen seconds it was down to three thousand million degrees, which had the effect of speeding up the annihilation of electrons and protons, but I don’t know why. This extra destruction produced more energy which had the effect of slowing the cooling process down but nevertheless cooling continued until it dropped to a mere one thousand million degrees, so damping down the zooming about activity. This allowed the protons and neutrons to form nuclei. (Am I allowed to ask why this was so? Anyhow, it was just as well, for our sake.)

But to continue - the first one was called deuterium (heavy hydrogen) of one proton and one neutron, followed by helium. There was much interaction until at the end of the first three minutes there were approximately 73% hydrogen and 27% helium plus the electrons left over from the phase of electron – positron annihilation. Then after a few hundred thousand years it was cool enough to allow the electrons to join up with nuclei to form atoms. (Of course, there were no years either because there was no sun to create diurnal rhythms, so it could just as well have been instantaneous at the time.)

This produced gasses which a theoretical gravity caused to form clouds, which then condensed into clumps to produce galaxies and stars. (All this marvellous prediction overlooks the fact that how mass and space came about is unknown.) One thing led to another, then after a long time and with much off-ing and on-ing, joining and splitting of bits and pieces, eruptions with much thundering and heaving, and lots and lots of time – hey presto! Here we are! It leaves me in awe of human capacity, ingenuity and dogged endeavour. However, let me point out that all this only accounts for about 5% of total matter. 95% of matter in the universe is unknown and maybe unknowable. (Cosmologists call it 'dark' matter or 'dark' energy.)

While ambling through the days, I am thinking things cosmic, due to the accident of buying that book. I find that these modern concepts of cosmology are as fascinating as fantasy. While marvelling at it all, I have a sneaky feeling that something, something vital, revealing, essential, has been denied, overlooked, lost. Though not a sceptic, I am a doubter; even of the logical or reasoned. I doubt for instance, the astronomer's interpretation of the red shift observed in light from distant galaxies as being the Doppler Effect. If it proves not to be, the theory of the expanding universe and the concomitant Big Bang might go down the gurgler. To a speculating scientist, a logical interpretation is apt to be taken as a truth, so the comfortable feeling of being a knower is enjoyed. Contrasted to this, a doubter is a non-knower for both proof and truth are regarded as species of rational thought and logic. To a doubter such as I am, proofs are provisional and truths are relative.

Whether this brilliant model is true or not, it makes marvellous thoughts possible. It can be inferred that the balance throughout the dynamic changes was achieved by the twin energies of creation and destruction producing the preservation of dynamic stability - (a trinity the Hindus call Brahma, Shiva and Vishnu) - and that change is brought about by one of them gaining or losing intensity. No matter how radical the change a dangerous and dynamic preservation has always been maintained. From the very beginning - though that state is beyond speculation - each phase follows apparently *inevitably. Nothing could be otherwise. If the events of the first three minutes were other than they were, the universe, our world and life would be other than it is – or perhaps would not be at all.* Everything in all galaxies here now was there then. Our bodies are star dust and our energies electric. Was it all haphazard and by chance or did the energy that informed the process have life 'in mind' and was therefore intelligent? Is it a mere accident that photons of sunlight have precisely the right energy to produce the chemical reactions essential to life in photosynthesis?

By some miraculous manipulations a temperature in which most organisms can function best, (about five to forty degrees) is maintained and nature regulates the balance of gases in the blanket under which all living things exist. Somehow, over the aeons the critical percentage of oxygen in the atmosphere has been maintained at twenty one percent. If it dropped too far below fifteen percent nothing except some anaerobic bacteria could live and nothing could burn. Too much above twenty one percent things would tend to spontaneously combust. Contrary to popular opinion, the ordinary is extraordinary

Thus the atomic processes at the beginning of creation must have been directed by the intention of life. One small change in the process and life would not have been possible.

I am grateful to have arrived at the last sentence in this book; one of the few easy to understand. To quote: 'The effort to understand the universe is one of the very few things that lifts human life a little above the level of farce and gives it some of the grace of tragedy.' *The writer cannot see that his effort does not lead to an understanding of the universe - just an understanding of a modern physicist's interpretation of it.*

As for life as it is now, Einstein had this to say:

> 'A human being is part of the whole called by us the 'Universe', a part limited in time and space. He experiences himself, his thoughts and feelings, as something separate from the rest – a kind of optical delusion of his consciousness. This delusion is a kind of prison for us, restricting us to our personal desires and to affections for a few persons nearest to us. Our task must be to free ourselves from this prison by widening our circle of compassion to embrace all living creatures and the whole of nature in its beauty. Nobody is able to achieve this completely, but the striving for this achievement is in itself a part of the liberation and a foundation for inner security.'
>
> Albert Einstein, *The New York Post,* 28 November 1972.

And from another great seer of another age cautioning humility at all theories, opinions and speculations –

Those who regard their knowledge as
ignorance have deep insight.
Those who regard their ignorance as
definite truth are deeply sick,

...This who return their mind to
simplicity are not sick, because
they know that their conceptual knowledge is not truth.
This is the secret of their health.'
(Tao Teh Ching of Lao Tzu)

TRYING TO MAKE SENSE OF THE SENSES

An investigation into the world of our senses reveals some startling facts, so fasten your seat belts- you are in for an amazing ride. First off, it shows that what we call 'the world' is only the senses functioning, because all the qualities we ascribe to our world of experience depends entirely of the nature of each sense. Imagine what sort of world you would inhabit if you had eight senses instead of five, or if you could see the ultraviolet or infrared spectrums – smell the smells a dog can or have the hearing of an owl - it would certainly not be the same world whose real existence you now accept and believe in. How our world would appear if we could see radio waves is beyond knowing. Our notions of the world cannot be separated from the limitations and acuity of the senses.

Sight can report only a minute portion of the electromagnetic spectrum and the others are similarly limited, so the totality of what actually *is* must remain unknown. That takes some chewing and might be as hard to digest as the corollary which is - *what they seem to report cannot be the qualities of an objective, solid, external reality, but merely the limitations of their own nature.* No real world as we know it? What nonsense you might think! Though these facts are contrary to common sense they have support from neurological science.

Let's take another look - consider it this way - if we took the reports of the senses as absolute truths our understanding of the Universe would still be back in the dark ages. According to sensory experience it is obvious that the sun orbits the earth, that the earth, though bumpy, is flat, that two upright poles a mile apart on a flat plane are parallel, that heavy things cannot be made to fly, that energy and matter are different, or that the earth is stationary in space and does not rotate. The testimony of the senses had to be transcended before the truth of all these things could be proved.

Another startling thing to try to get into our understanding is that the real location of everything is not 'out there'. The actual location of everything is 'in here' - our own brain. The best that can be done to explain these strange facts is to say that an unknown something produces vibrations that are read in the language of each of the five senses as digitally programmed blips in nervous tissue. There are no colours or shapes in the optic nerves, no sounds in the auditory nerves, no smells or tastes in the nerves of smell or taste, no smooth, rough, hot or cold in the nerves of touch – only blips travelling up the nerve fibres to the brain. We call the resulting electro-chemical events in the brain reality. It is the pattern of these blips in the brain that become the Universe. The brain is the greatest mystery in all creation. Maybe the nature of experience can never be fathomed. If this thought is new to you, stop and wonder about the implications.

Here is one; *sensory activity is not perception.* The action of the senses presents nothing but the bare sensation or chemical-electrical changes in tissues. They cannot present us with ready-made notions of objects, yet we derive from an excitation of nerve fibres and an electrical charge in certain minute brain cells, the complex notion of a world of objects and a million qualities of space, time, and causality. All these supposedly "external realities" are derived from purely internal changes. These facts possibly explain the phenomena of clairvoyance and clairaudience where knowledge is obtained directly beyond the range of eyes and ears. These faculties, like thought transference, must be due to changes in the sensitivity or structure of the brain. Another implication is that there is no such thing as ESP - Extra-Sensory-Perception, for in the final analysis all perception is sensory for the senses are in the brain, not the organs. EOP - extra-organ perception is more accurate, not extra sensory. Even in the ordinary experience of dreaming we experience a sensory world while the organs are asleep. These well documented phenomena show something else – what we call the senses is capable of extending their range into the paranormal.

We like to call all this transient weirdness of experience 'reality', but the only thing that can be called Reality is the unknown something everything is founded upon. Unlike everything we experience, it cannot be relative, does not come and go, is not subject to change, has no birth or death, and is most probably eternal, absolute and infinite. Every sensate creature from insect to mammal, micro organism to whale, reads in its own way the unfathomable and unknown Reality.

Even a verbal description of actuality is mind-boggling! The next weird fact to immerge is that you can only live in the Universe because the Universe lives in you! With further contemplation of the strangeness of life, joy, wonder, and awe flows through the mind like a silent river.

Of the five senses sight and hearing lead. They make known objects and events far distant from the organs. The others need actual contact, pressure to touch and molecules to taste and smell so they must have evolved first. Around our knowledge mysteries abound. I wonder how primitive eyes could be developed without knowledge of the possibility of sight and the presence of light. What is the explanation? Could it be that the senses are innate in the mind of the world and the organs are developed by torturous evolution from intrinsic knowledge of the possibility? Evolution then, is the process of the latent becoming potent, the potential actual. The famous Yogi Patanjali in his Yoga Sutras states that *Evolution is by the infilling of Nature.* The implications of these ideas are enormous, so if you are inclined to exercise your grey matter here is an opportunity.

Nearly half the sensory cells in the brain are dedicated to sight, the most precious sense of all. That magical faculty has led us to the most important developments in human culture. It started with cave art, signs and signals, then came painting and sculpture, apart from speech, the main means of communication and education in the Middle Ages. This culminated in reading the printed word, possibly the one most significant advance of all. Since the 19th century photography and the motion picture have been added, making revolutionary changes in knowledge, our perception of the world and ourselves. It is possibly the greatest agent of social change since the invention of printing, based entirely upon the senses of sight and hearing.

Mother nature tells the story...

"You have no idea how difficult it is to manufacture such a delicate thing as the eye. No wonder it is easily damaged and loses acuteness over the years. Please appreciate that it is one of evolution's most miraculous inventions - though so small compared to the liver for instance, though if you built a factory to duplicate the liver's functions, it would have to be three stories high and cover a half hectare of land and it still wouldn't work as well because all of its products would appear sequentially whereas the liver does it all at the same time. The kidneys are a marvel too, not to mention the feedback loops of the endocrine glands. The heart is nothing but a muscle in the vascular system and doesn't rate a mention in comparison. They are pretty easy to evolve compared to the eye. The eye is another order of things altogether.

Of your three senses it is the most spectacular. You think you have six senses but I count three because smell, taste and touch are really only variations of direct contact with molecules. Only hearing and sight read at a distance and of the two, sight is the more direct and caused me much more trouble. The ear was only a matter of using old-fashioned ideas from shells and hairs with a bit of ancient gristle on the outside to catch the vibes - but the eye! No recycling of old ideas there. It was so difficult, even for me, that I am not surprised that a few weaknesses happen.

Let me tell you; getting animals to see things was the most difficult thing. Light had been busy with algae to make enough oxygen so big critters could be made and there's no point in having critters that couldn't see where they were going, bumping into things and each other.

So, way back I had to make eyes for the Trilobites with a lens derived from calcium carbonate - after fractals, cohesion, symmetry, mobility, Arthropods, and sexual reproduction. It was just one darn thing after another. If I had any idea where a bit of fun with fire and volcanoes was going to lead, I would have blown the whole shebang up and saved myself millenniums of involvement with it all.

It took a long time to make tissues sensitive to light and they were not the lustrous orbs they are now; mirrors of the soul as your poets say. Then the skull had to be designed to take a pair of them. One eye would be no good at all. Talk about R&D! You have no idea. A few things are bound to be less than perfect. Building and maintaining an eco-system is no joke let me tell you, particularly when the top animal keeps mucking it up. One day I will get fed up with the whole complicated business, stop inflating and implode everything back to nothingness. I'd do it right now except that I am curious to see a few outcomes like will you lot clean up the mess you have made, or stop planning to populate other planets before you have learnt to live properly on this one; will you all reach cosmic consciousness; will the sea horse get a rider; will the 3.4 billion year old stromatolites in Western Australia start evolving – all the stories haven't been told yet. It's just as well I am timeless. Waiting isn't as issue. Now where was I? O yes, the eyes.

Now you humans might complain about gradual loss of vision as you grow older but think of how hard it is to make those intricate balls of jelly cushioned with fat, in holes in the skull supported by a complex system of little muscles all of their own – and most of the problems can be corrected with glasses anyhow.

I have to admit that I have made a few blunders over the millennia. No one is perfect. Even omniscience can get a bit frayed around the edges. Too much oxygen in what your scientists call the Cambrian era, and dinosaurs were far too big, and yes, the seed in the mango is too large, the flesh of the coconut too hard to get to and the tail of the brush turkey is the wrong way around. But all things considered, the eye is not one of the blunders."

Thanks for the insights Mum.

So much of the brain is involved with the senses and so are the listings of the meanings in the Macquarie dictionary - 20 ways the word sense is used apart from the words it is part of, such as sensual, senseless etc and 23 ways the word sight is used but only 14 for hearing. The eyes have it.

WHO DO I THINK I AM? THE ELUSIVE QUEST.

The popular TV series *Who do you think you are?* mirrors in its title the superficial opinions of our times. Yet so often an ancestor is unearthed the present descendent can identify with; the life stories sometimes uncannily similar. How can this be? Generation after generation, century after century, families are linked by common threads of entangled karma. If there is a person discovered way back when, to which a seeking descendent recognises someone similar to themselves, perhaps it is because they are the *same* person, generations apart.

It is a disaster of materialistic science to induce us to believe that we humans are merely mechanistic products of hereditary, environment and conditioning. Nonsense. There is nothing in my intrinsic personality that relates to anything in my past (as far as I can discover) or that I obtained by conditioning from either parent. I felt feelings and had thoughts and aspirations they could never have had and from childhood, intimations not derived from any external influence whatsoever. I am grateful that I have had two great advantages in life – a poor education and no religious indoctrination. As with most of us I suppose, who do you (other people) think I am, was more important than bothering about who I might be. My parents' selfless love must have been challenged by the fact that I sometimes seemed as alien as an extra-terrestrial. I wonder who they thought I was - but now the question in my old age is: *who do I think I am?*

But how to get the right answer? To reveal the truth, maybe the question needs investigating first, for I can see that the nature of the question determines the answer. Who do I think I am leads to one direction; who am I, what am I, leads to others? None of the possible answers satisfies me, for they all seem to hide the truth, begging the question; yes, but who am I really? So I suspect the real question should be, 'what is my intrinsic reality' or, what is my real nature? Questions that might lead to greater depths. On with the quest!

For religions and philosophy, our real identity has been a contentious issue and for me, one of some confusion over the years. Fortunately, various experiments to become a fixed person, well-rounded, solid and definite have failed. Having tried many, I must conclude at this point in time far removed from my first appearance on the planet that all attempts to be a definite somebody have failed. I suspect that any inquiry into identity is likely to get lost in a hall of mirrors, as the questions mentioned shows.

As everything one wants to know is available on Google, I thought it may have the answer. Googling my name has revealed the startling fact that that there are other Russell Atkinsons around the globe - but of course, with very different me's. Or so it seems – but what *is* this me?

It was very disconcerting to discover that actually, I, at least as a fixed, basic me, cannot be found. When I went searching for the live kernel inside the outside fruit I found nothing substantial at all. It was like peeling an onion down through layer after layer until the final one, then nothing. When nuclear scientists went into the atom, they discovered the same thing. Have we and this vast superstructure no solid foundation? Perhaps the insistence on there being a basic substance is a blemish that mars the quest.

To personality, ego, psyche, mind, whatever word is used to name these insubstantial entities, the core of being must appear to be a void – the nothing at the core of the onion. Empty, like the deep sleep state. Whatever it is, it is not a *thing,* so that is why thing-bound thinking cannot perceive it. Hmm... I am forced to suspect that as a me I am a product of my own imagination and have created my narrative as a person in the same way as an author does a protagonist in a story. Be that as it may, though my person is intimately linked to the story of my life, my history is not *me* – in the quest it is important not to assume that one is the other -so back to square one. On with the quest.

Here's one way of looking at it - all 'me's' are a personality – a word derived from the Greek *persona* meaning *mask.* So, it seems that searching for something real in the ever changing flux and moods, attitudes and proclivities of personality results in discovering nothing. (If you feel that this puts your being under threat, not to worry; the real meaning of nothing is *no –thing* so it should cheer you up to learn that at your core you are not just a mere thing.) Is there one major mask that is the prime knower of all the others? To me, this idea does not get the seal of a sensible approval, though in the metaphysical realm of the psyche a truth does not have to be reasonable. But it is reasonable to assume that every temporal mask of personality must be worn over a real face. On the level of ordinary experience we can be more rightly be called human becomings than human beings, yet all the vast range of becomings must require a consistent being. There must be the real *me* behind the various masks of personality. Or is there?

Maybe the subconscious awareness of being no-thing is the spur to the powerful urge to *be* somebody as we do in our youth; to feel secure in something solid like wealth, fame, possessions, or fixed opinions and beliefs. Perhaps the effort to create a fixed, constant, solid, consistent, respectable personality with a definite shape acceptable to the mores of the culture of one's times and gather possessions both material and psychological, is the cause of our various insanities. In one way or another, this dire malady inflicts almost everybody, manifesting signs from mild to acute, from egocentricity, insecurity, jealousy, intolerance, prejudice, bigotry, to vicious ambition, dogmatism and fanaticism. As these and their opposites are the fruit of our becomings, an enquiry into identity has ranged far beyond the personal.

This appears to be where the enquiry has led of its own flow, (with some help from the Upanishads) yet looking back over my personal narrative I see that I could be called a proselytiser. Hmm. Perhaps an aspect of the malady is manifesting for I see that what started out to be a light-hearted enquiry as per the TV series, is in danger of becoming a sermon. But this is what I often *do* – not what I *am,* for even a collection of proclivities, traits or characteristics could not be the intrinsic me. The question now is - are we just the sum of our parts? On with the quest.

Are there really people who are convinced that they are merely some sort of an adhesion of separate bits; body bits, mental bits, emotional bits, desires and urges, inherited and acquired and so on? If so, which bit is it that is aware of all the other bits? It is ridiculous to believe that one part of the flux of ever-changing everything can be the sole knower of everything else that is fluxing along with it. Even this persistent feeling of being a 'me' has no permanence in the range of human experience, for it becomes non-existent in deep sleep and becomes mysteriously reborn at waking. So whatever the real *knower* is, it must be other than the multiplicity in flux– something wholly other, over and above all conditioning, beyond ignorance and knowledge and consequentially, beyond our cognition. Naturally, it would appear to be a void. The void of unknowing. But a void can be a powerful thing. Zero means nothing but has the power to increase a one from ten to infinity.

And yet, in this weird old world what seems to be the 'unknown' is the only thing we can know for sure. It is the intuited conviction I AM. While everything we may imagine ourselves to be is only provisional and therefore subject to change, the only thing you can be really sure of is that you *definitely are*. No act of imagination or logic, no affirmation of non-being, nothing can change the intuition of I AM to I am not, for even to deny it is to affirm it. Everything we can know or imagine depends on our existence as **I AM.** It is the only emphatic constant. Yet this enigmatic reality cannot be known by the ordinary mind because it is neither a thing nor a no-thing, not knowable yet not unknown, indivisible, intangible, unconceivable, ineffable, undefinable. Therefore, truly spiritual. On this level we are all one identity. Even as seemingly separate me's we are not all that different. The range of ideas, proclivities, abilities and attitudes in our various personalities can form an infinite range of combinations, yet no matter how complex, the variations are of a limited range of psychological themes, as the vast range of music is based on only seven notes. *Viva la difference* as the French say. So finally, it seems that there is no reasonable answer to the question *who do I think I am?* for whatever I *think* I am, I am not. I am the existence that reveals everything else. We intuit I AM beyond everything we think we know. It is the fundamental consciousness that makes it possible to be aware of being alive, the only emphatic constant in the constant flux. So, I do not *think* I AM - I AM and that's that. So maybe it could be said that me is not I, but this hidden I is what lights the me – something like that.

The quest has brought us to the brink of nothing; zero – yet like the mathematical zero it is capable of creating infinity – in human terms, all that we know. Rather than a black void, the apprehension of the unknown at the core of our being is the fount of living beauty - for realizing our personality as a self-created phantom is a revelation producing humility, self-knowledge, levity and joy, while the realization of our universal identity is the fount of compassion and the living source of an uninvented morality and ethics. Acknowledging our simultaneous and fundamental identity is the fount of joy and wonder at racial differences as marvellous variations on a theme. It is all so simply possible when the mighty unknown is acknowledged. Marvellous, isn't it?

So, this is where the quest has led us, but you see, it has turned out to sound like a sort of sermon after all. O well, I can't help it; that's me.

THE TIME OF GREAT CONFUSION

The *Hua Hu Ching* from which these excerpts are taken is attributed to the legendary founder of Taoism, Lao Tzu, reputed author of the famous *Tao Teh Ching.* According to the traditional history, Lao Tzu was the emperor's librarian during the Chou dynasty, c 2,600 years ago. The *Hua Hu Ching* is a large work, including the principles of the I Ching, Tai Chi, Acupuncture and energy healing. These excerpts are only those relating to 'the time of great confusion' that Lao Tzu could see coming. They are taken from a book entitled *The Complete Works of Lao Tzu* by Ni Hua Ching and published in 1979. In the foreword Master Ni admits that few if any complete or accurate copies of the work exist in China today. It is only through the oral transmission of the *Hua Ha Ching* through many generations of Taoist masters, of which Master Ni is descended, that it has now become available to students.

Many of us in the 21st century have the same sort of feeling as did Lao Tzu. It is indeed a time of great confusion. What has Lao Tzu to say about it? (The teachings are in the form of a dialogue between the teacher and a student.)

❧

"My venerable teacher, will the people in the future generations in the time of great confusion be able to understand the truth?"

"Kind Prince, in future generations in the time of great confusion people will create many false truths and hold fast to their own blindness. They will persuade other people to follow them and be just as they are. They will even persecute the unbelievers and start wars against them ..... Because one departs from his own nature to search for something external, he overlooks the truth of his own being. To be is to be true. The muchness and suchness of truth is included in this very second. If you miss the truth of this moment a thousand galloping horses cannot keep up with it. The relative mind only creates conflicts, both within oneself and with others. One notion fights another notion. One time fights with another time. Life becomes full of contradiction misery and tragedy.... I

In the future humanity will overemphasize the intellectual element of the mind and disregard the intuitional. Instead of recognizing the wholeness of life, people will perceive life as having a worldly and spiritual aspect, both of which are separate and unrelated to each other. They will lose themselves amidst all the isolated fragments of conceptions and information and be the victims rather than the masters of their knowledge .... Human society will be pervaded by all kinds of slavery. Slavery will exist in all human relationships, but under different names and systems. If an individual is not a slave to his society, then he will be a slave to his family. If he is not the slave of his ambition, he will be the slave of his emotions. If he is not the slave of his desire, he will be the slave of his ego. The forms of slavery are multiform and may include the slavery to money, to a life of luxury, to social position, to religion, to an ideology, to the things one craves, to one's destiny, to one's biological drives ... the absolute Way will be available in all times and places as the way to transcend dualistic thinking.

.... The remedy for the people of the future in the time of great confusion will lie in the ancient wisdom of the integral way of life. The holistic way of life practiced by the ancient sages incorporated body, mind and spirit as one whole in all activities. Their education was broad and comprehensive and did not emphasize one element of their being while neglecting others. They did not seek special activities for their recreation; their work and recreation were one and the same. Their forms of exercise developed not only the body but the mind and spirit as well, through the harmonization of their internal energies. Their music functioned as a bridge between mind and spirit, not merely as an emotional release. Their leaders were chosen because they were outstanding models of virtue, not for their financial, diplomatic or military capabilities. Philosophy, science, and spiritual practices were incorporated as one whole."

"My venerable teacher, how may the people of the future era of great confusion deal with those troubled times?"

"The people of the future should not blindly accept the new, nor blindly reject the old. The new inventions which will appear may seem to be short cuts, but things of temporary convenience shall bring hidden trouble later. The future generations will need to reevaluate all old and new discoveries and inventions. This will ensure that there are useful and healthy creations according to the standard of the holistic way of life .... when the long age of confusion begins people will undertake important endeavors guided only by their ambition. To destroy one society for the sake of the growth of another society stems from the blind ambition of the ignorant leaders of the world. Argumentation and war is for the ignorant. Peace is the only way for one who knows the Truth."

"My venerable teacher, in the future time of great confusion will there be good men and women who have the opportunity to know the truth of immortality and who will succeed in breaking through their own cycles of life and death to become immortal?"

"In future generations, because people procreate as prolifically as the silkworm produces eggs, with little moral control or astrological awareness, there will inevitably be many disabled and sick individuals. The blind and ignorant multiplication of population degrades the quality of humanity. In future times there will appear collective murdering, slaughter, plagues and finally war in which all will perish. Because of the destructive tendencies of the vulgar world, this kind of end seems to be unavoidable .... The only people who will be able to save themselves are those who practice selflessness and follow the absolute Way of life. .... humanity has degraded itself generation after generation until at last, people have lost their Self-awareness. Finally, in their blindness, they will destroy both themselves and the world. This has happened on the human plane many times before and will happen again at the climax of human culture. So the new world must begin again with virtuous beings. Kind Prince do not be bothered by the future destruction. There is always a remedy when one embraces the absolute Oneness.

"My venerable teacher, in future generations during the time of great confusion, will the one who studies and practices this scripture be able to gain the absolute eye of Tao?"

"Kind Prince, the one who studies and practices this scripture will obtain the absolute eye of Tao which is the authentic insight into all Truth."

"My venerable teacher, should one live in seclusion and cultivate oneself in order to transcend all worldly troubles and pain? Or should one courageously take on the troubles and pain of worldly experiences as important elements in attaining enlightenment and absolute virtue?"

"King Prince, it is not a question of whether one should live in the seclusion or in the world. The question is this: Will one really achieve complete enlightenment and spiritual freedom, or will one become only partially enlightened? If one achieved only partial enlightenment, he may become clever, sharp-tongued, and so overly-sensitive that he is unable to bear the task of living in the real world. Or he may rush to establish his own teachings to impart to the world. In any of these instances, this person deviates from the Tao... In the future the streets will be full of half-enlightened, self-proclaimed teachers who will bring about much confusion. Any oddity, strangeness, or fanaticism goes against the absolute Way. The absolute Way values plainness of speech, dress and behavior as far more precious than that which is exciting, dazzling, and fashionable. By establishing honesty in every facet if life one may return to Simplicity. Excessiveness and extremisms is never practiced by those who follow the Way. Extravagant lifestyles, fancy food, and raucous music spoil the serenity of the mind and cause one's subtlety to become dull, one's life to become barren and one's spiritual unfolding to regress. The Truth is near when one leaves the mind. It is far away when one keeps thinking and doubting. Everything is ready when one is ready. Nothing is ready when one is not ready. Kind Prince, are you ready?

❧

The author of the *Hua Hu Ching* was the Taoist Master Ni Hua-Ching who migrated to California in the 60's. His translation of the *Tao Te Ching* and writing of the *Hua Hu Ching* show the influence of modern times and I suspect that there is much of Master Ni in the *Hua Ha Ching*. I wonder if his description of the time of great confusion are a little too apt for this century; or is it true that history repeats itself ad infinitum?

Judging by another quote from an ancient Taoist source, it is true indeed:

> *Produce! Get results! Make money! Make friends! Make changes! Or you will die of despair! Those who are caught in the machinery of power take no joy except in activity and change. Whenever an occasion for activity presents itself, they are compelled to act; they cannot help themselves. They are inexorably moved, like the machine of which they are a*

part. Prisoners in the world of objects, they have no choice but to submit to the demands of matter. They are pressed down and crushed by external forces, fashion, the market, events, and public opinion. Never in a whole lifetime do they recover their right mind. What a pity!

Chuang Tzu, Zen Master 300BC

The following quote is also disturbingly apt:

Never was there perhaps, more hollowness of heart than at present. We live in an atmosphere of hypocrisy throughout. A scornful superciliousness rules literature. The aim of all the litterateurs is to find something to make fun of. A lot of churches and sects – the most dismal phantasms I know of, usurp the name of religion. The depravity of the business classes in this country is not less than has been supposed, but infinitely greater. The official services, national, state and municipal in all their branches and departments except the judiciary, are saturated in corruption, bribery, falsehood, maladministration; and the judiciary is tainted. The great cities reek with respectable as much as nonrespectable robbery and scoundelisms. In fashionable life, flippancy, tepid amours, weak infedelism, small aims, or no aims at all; only to kill time. In business the one sole object is by any means, pecuniary gain. It is as if we were somehow being endowed with a vast and more and more thoroughly appointed body, and then left with little or no soul.

This was written in by Walt Whitman (1819-1892) an American poet famous for his vigorous verse in *Leaves Of Grass.*

And according to this quote it was worse centuries later:

'Religious, secular, or something in between, most Americans of the early 2000s shared some concern about a broad

range of threats to the nation's future: immorality, decadence, crime, terrorism, private and public corruption, moneyed politics, greed and luxury, and the stratification of wealth and power.' From Kevin Philip's book, American Theocracy.

Yet in the intervening decades perhaps no culture in any civilization has ever blossomed and boomed in a creative rush as has America and to varying degrees the rest of the world followed.

So what's to be learnt from these writings about these troublesome aspects of civilization? The history of humans seems to point to the dismal fact that every age has its time of great confusion. The very important difference is that what was once a local and limited plague of moral decline has become global; much of it institutionalized or promoted as entertainment or lauded as personal freedom.

Inundated with avalanches of bad news it is too easy to get a jaundiced view of the world. The other side gets little or no airing. - On the other hand,... the other story... every positive has a negative.... grey areas... vice versa... every negative has a positive... opposites are complementary... All these saying point to the fact that times of confusion overlay or are attended with its opposite of culture, morality and enlightenment. Walt Whitman would have been less critical with American culture in the decades that followed his death in 1892. After the Great Columbian Exhibition in Chicago in 1893 revolutionary ideas swept America from coast to coast and similar break-throughs in all fields of endeavour burgeoned in the UK and Europe as well, led by names still well known – Emerson, Edison, Tesla, Thoreau, the 'New Thought' poetess, Ella Wheeler Wilcox, Harriet Beecher Stowe, author of *Uncle Tom's Cabin,* led a renascence in the arts and sciences.

In the UK and Europe there was a similar resurgence of culture and science with other famous names, the Huxley's, Maxwell, Shaw, Marconi Rutherford with many others, and the

German philosophers and academics. But does what we deem to be the good outweigh what we call evil or the bad? I think not. In spite of the urge to optimism and the powerful belief in the inevitability of progress an overview of history inclines me to believe that there are constants within the ever-changing patterns, and I am reminded of the old French saying: *the more things change the more they stay the same.* The more something gets better the worse something else becomes. Every benefit is balanced with a downside; every downside with a benefit in the great law of compensation (and what one age deems to be good the next thinks bad.) So it is that religion has caused so much strife and conflict because it has done so much good; because science has done so much good it has caused so much bad and so it goes – every upside has a downside, and every downside has an upside; though it should be admitted that finding the upside of downsides is sometimes difficult. But yes, the good and the truth always outweighs and eventually surpasses the bad, lies and errors; if it were not so, civilisation would have rotted into oblivion millennias ago.

There is an old philosophical saying: *as above so below.* So, the cosmic law of compensation that keeps opposites in a dynamic balance in the macrocosm should be discernible in the microcosm – and so it is. It is called homeostasis. The biochemical aspects of physiology are fascinating, showing how temperature, acid-alkali and charge balance are kept within limits that are much more critical than cosmic ones. Many of the body's organs such as lungs, skin, and kidneys work together to keep the acid-alkali balance in the blood close to ph6. Too much each side of this the body collapses. Body temperature must be maintained between 36 and 37 degrees or collapse and death follows slight deviations. The temperature in a glass of chilled water rises to match the ambient temperature; a hot one cools down until it reaches the ambient temperature, showing how nature always attempts equalization of its forces. One can also reason in the reverse - *as below, so above* - hinting that there are cosmic forces or laws at play that keep all opposites in balance as in all animal bodies. This *as below so above* can be extrapolated into a most potent thought – the emphatic and persistent conviction of being a person living in a finite body implies the existence of a Cosmic Person whose body is the infinite cosmos. If this is so, it follows that we are personifications of cosmic forces and principles in an intimate relation.

So, what to do in the times of great confusion? The only action that can be taken to offset a time of great confusion is not to add to it, and live lives of integrity, virtue and simplicity such as was advised by Lao Tzu thousands of years ago. It was much the same as that offered in order to live harmonious lives by Moses, Christ, Mohamed, Buddha, Krishna and the sages and saints of all religions. However, ...

No religion worships bondage and slavery
no philosophy teaches them as the ideal.
No savant lauds error or ignorance,
no sage preaches hypocrisy and strife,
no science, conflict and division,
yet everywhere they flourish;
for many hear but few listen.

LET THERE BE LIGHT

Light, that reveals everything else, is usually ignored, unless one is an artist or photographer. We see *things* but not the light that reveals them, unaware that everything thus revealed conceals that which makes it all possible. As commonplace as light is, it is really mystical, magical and marvellous. It plays marvellous tricks. At night at the sink I can see a facsimile of the television screen, apparently located within the van in the carport, though it is actually in the lounge room behind me but mirrored in the kitchen window. I can still watch the TV screen though it is actually behind my back. Outside, in the carport, the long windows of the campervan shine with images of the kitchen bench and the colourful line of containers with the television screen superimposed. They are bright shadows of the actual.

Far away, old father sun, beaming in a cloudless sky, waves its light through the stratosphere, down into the biosphere, through the sunroom windows, across the sunroom, through the bedroom window, then across the room to make a shadow picture of a tree on the wall above my head. In summer the wall vibrates with a brilliant patch of light shadowed with the fine leaf-tips from the tall tree way down the backyard. Moving pictures in slow motion yet. Such is light. It is the creator of illusions and mirages. And shadows. As the sun moves from dawn to dusk, shadows of the trees outside make pictures on the walls of different rooms.

I got to wondering: are shadows *things*? Can a shadow, so insubstantial, be given the status of *something*? I suspect that they have a reality as real as things. The fact that they are less substantial means nothing, for most crucially important aspects of our life have no substance, such as intelligence, love, sympathy, or feelings. I discovered that I could not photograph a shadow without also including something substantial, like a wall, even if it is only an anonymous surface. Like light itself, the surface is ignored and only the shadow is seen. This is identical to what happens when we read a book. We are only aware of the letters and words, not the paper. This is also similar to our experiences, for we are only aware of the temporal moments of experience, shadows on the everlasting background behind them, as Plato suggested with his shadows on a cave wall allegory. Judging by the many ways shadows are referred to, from politics to poetry, simile and metaphor, they have a major place in the human psyche - so they are real enough.

Seeing that the sun gives us light and light gives us food and food sustains life, sun worship makes a lot of sense. Pagans did and Egyptians too for a time. The brave pharaoh Akhenaton in the 14th century founded a religion worshiping Aten, the sun. It made too much sense to be popular so his successor Tutankhamen disbanded it. Hindus revere the sun, not only as the giver of life but as the giver of enlightenment. The Gayatri mantrum chanted daily for thousands of years is a hymn to the Being in the sun for enlightenment, acknowledging the connection of light with consciousness. Enlightening all experience, every embodied being shines a spark from the light of cosmic consciousness, just as objects are revealed by sun light. Actually, light and sight make each other, for what we call light is but a minute portion of the electromagnetic spectrum the eyes can respond to. If we could see beyond ultraviolet and infrared we would be living in a different world. If we were sensitive to most of the spectrum there wouldn't be a solid world at all. Yet the visual range can be extended, for some rare human beings have so sensitised their brain cells that they can see auras, thoughts and spirits. What we call reality is actually the limitation of the senses. It's all very weird, this seeing and being.

Naturally enough, physicists have always been concerned with light and now applaud themselves with having measured its velocity in a vacuum at 299792458 metres per second or if you would rather, 186000 miles per second. It seems that human ingenuity has no limits, though understanding does, for this is not so. For light has no metres, miles or seconds and occurs in a vacuum only when subjected to human manipulation. Once again we have reduced the eternal and infinite into our little measures, showing how it is possible to hide the truth with facts. Nor is light the absolute constant as once thought for experiments with what physicists call entanglement reveals immediate action at a distance and immediate means no time at all. To describe it in the clumsiest terms, imagine two dice in Sydney, both turned so that the number one is uppermost. Then take one dice to Perth, number one uppermost. If one dice is turned so that the number two is uppermost, the other automatically has the number two uppermost as well. Instant is faster than the speed of light. Of much early contention it has now been done with charged photons. Einstein hated the idea. It's a great puzzlement.

Scientists have been much concerned with the speed of light but no one bothers about the speed of dark. I don't know why. Dark must have been there before because God said "Let there be light!" I suppose that the dark was still there but it would have been a lot easier to see.

First Light

The spirit of life itself, you come with each new day's rebirth,
Gentler than snowflakes drifting, silent as smoke, slow as snails,
Inevitable as gravity or moments, you seep
At each new day's birth into my slow waking.
Slowly as you come, my world emerges
from out the mists of dreaming,
But upon my closed eyes are not yet come to being.
Opened, I see them all dimly, waiting in the gloom to fully be
And grow bold and precise as you swell
slowly into this little room,
You, magic spirit of all seen things.

Why are you so humble that I see through
you as though you were not there?
Why do you hide behind brightness
So I move through you busy doing,
Never knowing, that like a fish in water,
I live in you? And like a sparkle off water, you live in me?
Your brightness dazzles. I am blinded by light.
Because you are so humble, making eyes so you can, unseen,
Revel in colours, form and space - or hide behind shadows.

Bright spirit of all shining things, hiding
behind the dazzle of the sun,
You are far away yet here, soul of my eyes and eyes of my soul.
Because you are there, far away,
This little awareness is here, watching you coming,
And though you shine forever, and my light is but a blink,
Together we light the world.

www.ingramcontent.com/pod-product-compliance
Lightning Source LLC
Chambersburg PA
CBHW071016180726
48291CB00004B/1484
* 9 7 8 1 9 2 2 2 7 0 8 0 1 *